Savages

CHRISTOPHER HAMPTON

Savages

FABER & FABER
3 Queen Square London

First published in 1974
by Faber and Faber Limited
3 Queen Square London WC1
Printed in Great Britain by
Latimer Trend & Company Ltd Plymouth
All rights reserved

ISBN 0 571 10348 0 (paper covers)
ISBN 0 571 10437 1 (hard bound edition)

All rights whatsoever in this play are strictly reserved and applications for permission to perform it, etc. must be made in advance, before rehearsals begin, to Margaret Ramsay Ltd., 14a Goodwin's Court, St. Martin's Lane, London W.C.2

For K.B.
and for friends in Brazil

INTRODUCTION

On 23rd February 1969, the *Sunday Times* Colour *Magazine* published an article by Norman Lewis called 'Genocide', which dealt with the destruction of the Brazilian Indians. Among the many appalling examples of systematic extermination discussed by Mr. Lewis and ranging from the sixteenth century to the present day was one which involved the slaughter of large numbers of the Cintas Largas tribe, supervised by one Francisco de Brito, 'general overseer of the rubber extraction firm of Arruda and Junqueira of Juina-Mirim near Aripuanã, on the river Juruena' in the early sixties.

'It was seen as essential', Mr. Lewis writes, 'to produce the maximum number of casualties in one single devastating attack, at a time when as many Indians as possible would be present in the village, and an expert was found to advise that this could best be done at the annual feast of the "Quarup". This great ceremony lasts for a day and a night, and under one name or another it is conducted by almost all the Indian tribes whose culture has not been destroyed. The "Quarup" is a theatrical representation of the legends of creation interwoven with those of the tribe itself, both a mystery play and a family reunion attended not only by the living but by the ancestral spirits. These appear as dancers in masquerade, to be consulted on immediate problems, to comfort the mourners, to testify that not even death can disrupt the unity of the tribe.

'A Cessna light 'plane used for ordinary commercial services was hired for the attack, and its normal pilot replaced by an adventurer of mixed Italian-Japanese birth. It was loaded with sticks of dynamite—"bananas" they are called in Brazil—and took off from a jungle airstrip near Aripuanã. The Cessna arrived over the village at about midday. The Indians had been preparing themselves all night by prayer and singing, and now they were all gathered in the open space in the village's centre. On the first run packets of sugar were dropped to calm the fears of those who had scattered and run for shelter at the sight of the 'plane. They had opened the packets and were tasting the sugar ten minutes later when it returned to carry out the attack. No-one has ever been able to find out how many Indians were killed, because the bodies were buried in the bank of the river and the village deserted.'

It is this incident which forms, and which I knew as I read the article would form, the climax of this play. How this insistent image developed over the next four years into the finished play is a long and irrelevant story I need not go into here, except to mention that it involved first a realisation that it would be impossible to deal with the 'Indian problem' at all adequately without taking into account the current political situation, and second a journey to Brazil, which confirmed much of what I had researched in England, as well as providing one or two of those revelations which seem so obvious in hindsight, notably that the average urban Brazilian has far too many difficulties in his life to allow himself the luxury of worrying about the Indian of the interior, of whose existence he is in fact largely ignorant.

The purpose of this Introduction is to sketch in a minimum of background information to the play. Separate sections will deal with the differences between this, the full original version of the play, and the first stage production at the Royal Court and subsequently at the Comedy Theatre; and with the ceremony of the 'Quarup', or at least those portions of it which we decided to portray on the stage.

The legends spoken by West are based, respectively, on myths of the Kayapo-Gorotire, Macuxi, Arekuna, Xipaya, Xerente and Tukuna tribes. Two of them ('The Origin of Music' and 'The Life After Death') I found in Vol. 11 of the immense *Mythology of All Ages* (ed. Alexander), and the rest are from the first two volumes of Claude Lévi-Strauss's *Mythologiques—Le Cru et le Cuit* and *Du Miel aux Cendres*. The geographical area covered by these tribes is enormous—from the Xingu to the Colombian border to and perhaps even across the borders of Venezuela and Guyana—but I felt no necessity to choose myths from a specific area of Brazil, any more than I felt restricted when I was informed by various anthropologists and friends that strictly speaking the Cintas Largas tribe could not have been performing a 'Quarup', as this is a ceremony limited to the Xingu area. The point is, as Norman Lewis says, that 'this great ceremony . . . *under one name or another* . . . is conducted by almost all the Indian tribes whose culture has not been destroyed'; and since what is in question is not only the fate of individual tribes, but the survival of an entire race, I haven't hesitated to sacrifice scrupulous anthropological accuracy to what seemed to me to be most appropriate dramatically.

As to the political background of the play it is perhaps enough to say that an American-backed military coup took place in Brazil on 1st April 1964; that a serious urban guerrilla movement under the leadership of Carlos Marighela of the A.L.N. (Ação Libertadora Nacional) was established in 1968; that the military dictatorship consolidated its position in December 1968 with the notorious Fifth Institutional Act, designed to suppress all political and civil opposition; that between September 1969 and December 1970 ambassadors and embassy officials from the U.S.A., Japan, West Germany and Switzerland were kidnapped and exchanged for varying numbers of political prisoners; and that the urban guerrilla movement began slowly to fall apart after Marighela had been killed by the police in November 1969. The West-Carlos section of the play is set in early 1971—in other words at a time when intense police pressure and the widespread use of torture was undermining and destroying the revolutionary movement: the event is fictional but the circumstances and outcome are, I think, not too unlikely. By 1972 the urban guerrilla movement was said to be crushed and finished, and, to judge by the methods used by the government (Amnesty International's report of September 1972 listed the names of 1,081 victims of torture), this, if true, is not altogether surprising. However, the *Observer* carried a report in March 1973 of extensive rural guerrilla activity in the states of Mato Grosso, Pará and Goiás.

As I said above, the initial inspiration for the play came from Norman Lewis's article in the *Sunday Times*: but its actual execution would have been impossible without the help of numbers of people both here and in Brazil, who provided me with much of the basic information, as well as pointing out factual inaccuracies in the completed play so diligently that any mistakes remaining are purely my own. However, to draw up a list of acknowledgements in the usual way, as I would like to have done, is impossible. As long as the situation remains as it is in Brazil (and it has so far, alas, shown no signs of modifying) it seems to me that it would be unwise to name the people who helped me most—especially those who were so kind to me in Brazil, those who would have arranged for me to visit the Xingu Indian Park through official channels, had it not suddenly seemed more prudent not to do anything through official channels, and those who arranged for me to see a film of the remnants of a now almost extinct tribe no less horrifying than the film of the survivors of Belsen. Above all, I would like to have been able to thank, other than privately, the anthropologist who helped me perhaps more than anyone else while I was writing the play (the account of the Beiços-de-Pau tribe in Scene Eighteen, for example, is adapted from his diaries) and who worked with the director during rehearsals of the play to give the scenes with the Indians a richness and authenticity we could otherwise never have achieved. I am sorry not to be able to thank those who helped me in a less oblique way: but I would rather take the risk of appearing ungrateful than the greater risk of embarrassing anyone with my thanks.

CHRISTOPHER HAMPTON

NOTES ON THE FIRST PRODUCTION

More than any of my other plays, *Savages* is a director's play; and I have decided to publish here the full original version of the script with a list (below) of the cuts which were made first at the Royal Court and then at the Comedy Theatre, not because I disagreed with the decisions made by the director, Robert Kidd—on the contrary I endorsed them all, with only one exception (see below), which, even for such a long and fruitful collaboration as ours has been, shows an unusual degree of harmony in a notoriously sensitive area—but because any director of any future production of the play will want to make his own decisions, depending on his own inclinations and, as likely as not, on the resources of the theatre, about what to include and what to leave out.

Scene One, p. 23: Fire regulations made the first and the last scenes of the play impossible to realise as they were imagined. This meant that my original intention which was to open and close the play with the image of fire—first as the Indians use it, as a central element of their ceremony, finally, as the pilots use it, to destroy that ceremony—had to be abandoned. This had a greater effect on the last scene than on the first: and I'm not sure that the solution we arrived at for the end of the play, which was to raise the frontcloth on the pile of Indian bodies and leave it at that, was not simpler and more effective than what I had intended. As to the first scene, it was played at the Royal Court as written (except that the logs in the fire were of course glowing rather than blazing) while at the Comedy the Indians were dispensed with altogether and the play opened with West simply speaking the legend on a bare stage. There were two reasons for this: first the Comedy stage has no trap (the method used for disposing with the 'fire' at the Royal

Court) and second (to make a virtue of necessity) it was felt that since there was no corresponding image of fire in the final scene of the play, there seemed no really pressing reason to have one at the beginning.

My original intention in this and in all the 'legend' scenes (for what I imagined to be purely practical reasons) was that West would not actually be present during the scenes but would only be heard as a voice-over reciting the legends. It was Paul Scofield who suggested that this would not be a good idea for a number of reasons, not the least of which, as I came to realise, was that it would have prevented him from adding the innumerable subtleties and refinements which accumulate in his performance during a play's run. This was only the first of very many great contributions Mr. Scofield made to the play.

Scene Five, pp. 35–7: The two lines spoken by Crawshaw during the scene between the General and the Attorney General ('Some months later.' and 'Later still.') were omitted from the production. Instead the passage of time in the General/Attorney General scene (which was played in front of a huge flag of Brazil) was marked by brief snatches of the Brazilian national anthem, during which the General and the Attorney General turned to salute the flag. The Brazilian national anthem also opened and closed the scene, covering the entrance and exit of the actors, the flying in and out of the flag, etc.

Scene Five, p. 38–9. A cut was introduced when the play moved to the Comedy

    from: WEST: 'Well that may be what happens, Miles . . .'

      to: CRAWSHAW: '. . . they keep saying they want to get rid of it in their speeches.'

Scene Six, p. 41: The first three speeches of this scene were cut, as was the following exchange:

    WEST: 'Why are they sending you to Cuba, aren't you good enough?'

    CARLOS: 'This is none of your business, Mr. West.'

This was because the director felt that the line: WEST: 'So you're the bastard.' made a far stronger opening to the scene.

Scene Seven, pp. 43–6: It was felt during rehearsals at the Royal Court that this scene, isolated as it is in the first act and lacking a clear conclusion was likely to be confusing to the audience. Accordingly a cut was made from:

PEREIRA: 'Luckily before long the plane came over . . .'
(*p. 45*)

to: PEREIRA: 'Shoot and no questions asked.' (*p* 46)

—and the remainder of the scene was moved to the second act (the present Scene Fourteen), so that the two Pereira scenes were played as one scene. This worked well, I felt, and consequently I was disappointed (this was the one area of disagreement referred to above) when the play moved to the Comedy and the decision was taken to omit the Pereira scenes altogether.

Scene Eleven,

p. 57: Cut from: PENN: 'I don't want you to think they're not free to come and go.'

to: PENN: '. . . I make the necessary arrangements.'

p. 58: Cut from: PENN: 'You know, when I first came to Latin America . . .'

to: PENN: '. . . so they couldn't be more helpful.'

p. 59: Cut from: PENN: 'Then, after a time, Kumai came to me . . .'

to: PENN: '. . . and had become involved with a girl . . .'

To replace this was a link passage:

PENN: 'Now what happened was that Kumai had been paying less and less attention to his wife and eventually I discovered he had become involved with a girl . . .'

Scene Fourteen, p. 68: See note on Scene Seven above.

Scene Seventeen, p. 76: This scene, which, like the Pereira scenes and the bombing scene, was based on material from Norman Lewis's article proved impossible to stage adequately at the Royal Court and was omitted.

Scene Twenty-Two, p. 85: See note on Scene One, above. The scene, as it was played at the Royal Court, was as follows:

The frontcloth rises to reveal a bloody heap of Indian bodies.

Silence.
An animal cry. Silence.
BLACKOUT *and* FINAL CURTAIN.

C.H.

A NOTE ON THE QUARUP

The Quarup is the principal ceremony of the Indians of the Xingu. It is not necessarily an annual event but may be held in any year during which a chief or person of chiefly birth has died. Not that it is a funeral ceremony in any conventional Western sense of the term: for, apart from its social importance as a gathering together of all the neighbouring tribes, one of its central events is the bringing out of seclusion of the young girls who have menstruated for the first time since the previous Quarup, who have been strictly confined since their menstruation, and who are now ready for marriage with their betrothed. This makes of the Quarup a celebration of rebirth as well as a lament for the dead, a ceremonial of a richness and subtlety to which no brief account can do justice, a ritual drama of regeneration.

The host tribe spends weeks preparing for this—sending out messengers to invite all the neighbouring tribes, clearing campsites for them and gathering enough food to feed them when they arrive. The day before the Quarup is spent setting up and decorating the Quarup posts, which represent those who have died, and which are decorated until they resemble the human body, at which point, in the eyes of the participants, they actually become those who are being mourned. In addition to this, there is dancing and flute-playing, and the members of the tribe decorate their own and each other's bodies.

During the night, as the mourners sit watching and lamenting the dead, representatives from the tribes camped round the village one by one rush into the village to steal firebrands in order to light their own fires.

The next day, the main ceremony unfolds. The messengers go out and lead the chiefs of each tribe into the centre of the village—and when they have taken their places, their tribesmen rush into the village, and the wrestling tournament begins with the strongest members of the host tribe each challenging the champion of one of the visiting tribes. This leads into a more general, less formal series of wrestling bouts, and then, after an exchange of gifts, the girls are brought out of seclusion, walking behind a kinsman of the dead chief, carrying a gourd cup containing 'pequi' nuts (a symbol of fertility), which they empty on the ground in front of the visiting chiefs. This is followed by general feasting and then by a dance in which pairs of flute-players (playing the special ten-foot Quarup flutes) followed by pairs of the now released girls visit each hut in the village in turn. After further celebration, speeches and a final distribution of gifts by the host tribe, the visiting tribes depart, leaving the host tribe to take the Quarup posts down to the lagoon at dusk and float them out until they sink and join the spirit village at the bottom of the lagoon.

The next morning, the chief gives every member of his tribe a new name.

C.H.

CHARACTERS

ALAN WEST

MRS. WEST

CARLOS ESQUERDO

MILES CRAWSHAW

GENERAL

ATTORNEY GENERAL

AN INVESTIGATOR

ATAIDE PEREIRA

MAJOR BRIGG

THE REVD. ELMER PENN

KUMAI

A pilot, a co-pilot, Indians, guerrillas, etc.

The bombing of the Cintas Largas tribe during the performance of their funeral ritual took place in 1963; and the confession of Ataide Pereira was recorded shortly after this by Padre Edgar Smith, S.J.

The rest of the play is set in Brazil in 1970-1.

Most of the characters in this play are fictitious: most of the events are not.

The play was first performed at the Royal Court Theatre on 12th April, 1973. The cast was as follows:

ALAN WEST	Paul Scofield
MRS. WEST	Rona Anderson
CARLOS ESQUERDO	Tom Conti
MILES CRAWSHAW	Michael Pennington
GENERAL	Leonard Kavanagh
ATTORNEY GENERAL/INVESTIGATOR	Gordon Sterne
ATAIDE PEREIRA	Glyn Grain
MAJOR BRIGG	A. J. Brown
CHIEF/BERT	Frank Singuineau
THE REVEREND ELMER PENN	Geoffrey Palmer
KUMAI	Terence Burns
PILOT	Leonard Kavanagh
CO-PILOT	Glyn Grain
INDIANS	George Baizley
	Lynda Dagley
	Thelma Kidger
	Donna Louise
	Eddy Nedari
	J. C. Shepherd

Directed by Robert Kidd
Designed by Jocelyn Herbert and Andrew Sanders
Lighting by Andy Phillips
Presented by the Royal Court Theatre and Michael Codron

'The "Indian problem" in Latin America is in its essence a problem of the economic structure of the national and international capitalist system as a whole.'

ANDRE GUNDER FRANK—*Capitalism and Underdevelopment
in Latin America*

'. . . il s'ensuit que la morale immanente des mythes prend le contrepied de celle que nous professons aujourd'hui. Elle nous enseigne, en tout cas, qu'une formule à laquelle nous avons fait un aussi grand sort que "l'enfer, c'est les autres" ne constitue pas une proposition philosophique, mais un témoignage ethnographique sur une civilisation. Car on nous a habitué dès l'enfance à craindre l'impureté du dehors.

'Quand ils proclament, au contraire, que "l'enfer, c'est nousmême", les peuples sauvages donnent une leçon de modestie qu'on voudrait croire que nous sommes encore capables d'entendre.'

CLAUDE LÉVI-STRAUSS—*L'Origine des Manières de Table*

One

Bare stage. In the centre, five or six blazing torches inclined towards each other to form a pyramid with a single head of flame. The theatre is entirely lit by this. Indian music, flutes, drums, chanting. Shadowy forms.

After a time, WEST *appears. As he speaks,* INDIANS *enter, one by one, from the wings, through the auditorium. Each takes a torch and returns with it the way he came.*

WEST: Origin of fire.
    In the old days men ate raw flesh
    And had no knowledge of fire.
    Also they had no weapons
    And hunted the game with their bare hands.

    A boy went hunting one day with his brother-in-law.
    They saw a macaw's nest up perched on a cliff-ledge.
    They built a ladder and the boy climbed up to the ledge.
    In the nest were two eggs.
    The boy took them and threw them down to his
      brother-in-law
    But in the air they turned into jagged stones
    Which as he went to catch them cut his hands.
    He was very angry.
    He thought the boy was trying to kill him.
    He took the ladder down broke it and went away.

    The boy was on the ledge for many days and nights
    Dying slowly of hunger
    Eating his own excrement
    Until one day the jaguar passed by
    With his bow and arrows

And seeing a shadow cast ahead of him on the ground
Looked up and saw the boy.
The jaguar mended the ladder helped the boy down
Took him back to his home and revived him
Feeding him cooked meat.

The jaguar loved the boy and treated him as his son
Calling him the foundling
But the jaguar's wife was very jealous of him
And when the jaguar was away she never missed a chance
To scratch him or to knock him over.
The boy complained to the jaguar that he was always
    frightened
So the jaguar gave him a bow and arrow
And taught him how to use them.
The next time the jaguar's wife attacked him
He shot an arrow at her and killed her.

The boy was terrified by what he had done.
He took his bow and a large piece of cooked meat
And escaped into the jungle.
After many days wandering he reached his own village
And told his people all the things that had happened to
    him
Showing them the meat and the bow.
The men were very excited by his discoveries
And they set off on an expedition to the jaguar's home
To steal his weapons
And to steal his fire.

What you take from people
They will never find again.
Now the jaguar has no weapons
Except his hatred for man.
He eats no cooked meat
But swallows the raw flesh of his victims.
And only the reflection and the memory of fire
Burn in his eyes.

(*Silence. The last torch has vanished. Embers. A strange cry in the darkness.*)

BLACKOUT

Two

A comfortable bedroom with twin beds. WEST *and* MRS. WEST *are in evening dress,* WEST *struggling with his bow-tie,* MRS. WEST *ready, waiting.*

WEST: God. I can never get these things to work.

MRS. WEST: You've had enough practice.

WEST: I know. What's the matter with it? I keep meaning to get one of those ones on an elastic strap. There we are. (*He makes a final adjustment, considers it in the mirror.*) Jesus, it looks ludicrous.

MRS. WEST (*sighing*): Start again. Concentrate.
   (*He does so.*)

WEST: Look, do we have to go to this thing?
   (MRS. WEST *turns away, ignoring him.*)
   Mm? Do we?

MRS. WEST: I don't know why you always say that. You know perfectly well we have to. At least, I don't have to. You have to. That's the only reason you're going in the first place, because you have to. So why you always say that, I don't know.

WEST: All right, there's no need to, I was just asking. (*Pause.*) I suppose there's always a remote chance there might be someone amusing or interesting there, never let it be said I'm not an optimist. That's better. (*He inspects himself in the mirror.*) No, it's not, it's worse.

MRS. WEST: It'll do.

WEST: No, it'll come undone.

MRS. WEST: We're going to be late.

WEST: What you mean is, we're not going to be early. I can't think why you have this passion for always wanting to be the first person there. All that happens is you hear your name spoken so often you begin to think there's at least six of you, and you run through all your small talk before the soup. I won't be a minute.

(*He undoes his tie again and turns to the mirror. As he does so, the door bursts open and three young men enter. They are all wearing rubber Walt Disney masks. Two of them are holding sub-machine-guns, the third,* CARLOS, *a pistol fitted with a silencer.*)

CARLOS: Mr. West?

WEST: Erm, er, no, I don't think so, no. Why?

(CARLOS *looks down at something in his hand and back at* WEST.)

CARLOS: I know you are Mr. West. Please put your hands up.

WEST (*doing so*): Oh.

CARLOS: Mrs. West.

MRS. WEST: Yes.

CARLOS: Please lie face down on the floor and put your hands behind your back.

(*She does so.* CARLOS *gestures and one of the others lays his gun down, produces rope, binds and gags her.*)

WEST: What is this?

CARLOS: Rag week.

(WEST *is nonplussed by this reply. With one hand he plucks at his tie.*)

Keep your hands still, please. (*Pause.*) Are you armed?

WEST: Of course not.

CARLOS: Right. Now you are to come with us. Our car is parked just outside the front door. You must walk just in front of me, on my left, sort of arm in arm. If you make any disturbance I shall shoot you more or less in the liver. Now. Do your tie up.

(WEST *fumbles hopelessly with his tie.*)

WEST: Easier said than done.

CARLOS: Do it!

(WEST *tries to. Time passes.*)

WEST: Be with you in a minute.

BLACKOUT

Three

A dark, dingy bedroom with a single bed. WEST *is lying on it, tied to the frame, a black canvas hood over his head. He sits up with a start, in so far as this is possible, when* CARLOS *comes into the room, holding a piece of paper.*

CARLOS: How are you?

WEST: Incredibly uncomfortable.

CARLOS: Yes. I'm sorry about this. I hope before the end of the day we'll be able to arrange something more satisfactory. Handcuffs.

WEST: Sounds wonderful.

CARLOS: But we're very busy at the moment.

WEST: Think nothing of it.

CARLOS: I've come to explain why this has happened to you.

WEST (*muffled*): Does it matter?

CARLOS: I beg your pardon.

WEST: Does it matter?

CARLOS: Well, it matters to us. And so, I suppose, in the circumstances, it matters to you as well. (*Pause.*) We are members of the M.R.B., the Movimento Revolucionario Brasileiro, and we have kidnapped you in order to achieve certain political aims. We have asked for the release of twenty-five political prisoners . . .

WEST: Twenty-five?

CARLOS: Yes.

WEST: Is that all?

CARLOS: Well, yes.

WEST: But you got forty for that German.

CARLOS: Yes, but he was the ambassador . . .

WEST: And seventy for the Swiss ambassador . . .

CARLOS: You don't think we've asked for enough?

WEST: No, I'm sure Her Majesty's Government will feel most affronted.

27

CARLOS: Well . . .

WEST (*muffled*): They probably take it as some sort of slight . . .

CARLOS: What?

WEST: I say they're probably annoyed you didn't kidnap the ambassador.

CARLOS: The security . . .

WEST: *I'm* annoyed you didn't kidnap the ambassador.

CARLOS: The security arrangements have become far more efficient recently.

WEST: You can't be speaking of the British Embassy.
  (*Brief silence.*)

CARLOS: We have asked, as I say, for the release of twenty-five prominent political prisoners, together with a safe conduct and facilities for flying them to Cuba. Then we have asked for 100,000 dollars, which is merely a formality, because, as you know, these people would rather give us their mothers than part with any real cash, so that's a kind of bargaining point. Finally, we've demanded, which is very important to us, that our manifesto (*he indicates his piece of paper*) is broadcast on TV and radio and released by the national and foreign press. I'm going to read it to you.

WEST: Don't.

CARLOS: No?

WEST: No, don't.

CARLOS: Well, we think it's very important for you to know and understand why we've done this to you, which is not a thing we like to do to anybody, you know? (*He reads some of the manifesto quickly through to himself, muttering.*) Hmm, hmm, yes, I'll miss out the first bit, this is about the heart of it, I think. 'We wish to draw the attention of the world to the fact that with the passing of the Institutional Acts, and in particular the fifth Institutional Act of 13th December 1968, the military dictatorship has transformed itself into the most regressive and repressive government anywhere in the world . . .'

WEST: Oh, really!

CARLOS: 'The measures it has introduced include:
  'The suspension of all political rights and banning of all

28

political parties except for the hired lackeys of the official opposition.

'The imposition of blanket censorship and the silencing of all opposition newspapers by intimidation and compulsory withdrawal of advertising.

'The promulgation of a law whereby "non-conformity" although nowhere defined, is described as a crime against the State.

'The expulsion of one-quarter of the officer corps.

'The appointment of government stooges as labour leaders and the stipulation that only candidates approved by the political police may stand in union elections.

'The reorganisation of the Supreme Court and the dismissal of those of its judges who expressed dissent. The suspension of habeas corpus.

'The cowardice and cynicism of the military dictatorship extends from the smallest and most ludicrous details, such as the replacement of the official Senate historian . . .'

WEST: Have they done that?

CARLOS: Yes, they have.

WEST: Good God.

CARLOS: '. . . the replacement of the official Senate historian, to the most cruel and squalid barbarities such as the reintroduction in September 1969, after seventy-five years of abolition, of the death penalty, to give spurious legality to the murders of Carlos Marighela, Mario Alves, Joaquim Camara Ferreira and countless other comrades in the struggle against Fascism.

'The military dictatorship has lined its pockets by selling our country to the interests of U.S. capitalism, which it has allowed to exploit our resources and steal our land, while our people starve and suffer all the miseries of poverty and unemployment. Meanwhile, anyone who utters the merest whisper of protest risks joining the 12,000 political prisoners, including university professors, doctors, writers, students, priests and nuns, at present suffering detention and brutal torture in the regime's jails and concentration camps. Anyone who doubts this should visit the Department of

Political and Social Order, where the corridors stink of
burnt flesh, or confront the thugs of the Death Squad,
whose hands are wet with innocent blood.

'This is what we are fighting against, comrades, and we shall
fight, if necessary, to the death.

'Death to U.S. imperialism!

'Down with the military dictatorship!'

That's all.

WEST: Quite enough.

CARLOS: What do you think?

WEST: I could quibble with your economic analysis.

CARLOS: This is not an analysis. This is a simple expression of
the truth.

WEST: Well, I suppose you could look at it that way.

CARLOS: We do.

WEST: Well, what the hell do you expect me to say about it? It
may be true or it may not be, and if it is I'm very sorry
about it, but it's nothing to do with me.

CARLOS: It is now.

WEST: Look, why don't you go away?

CARLOS: First I have to tell you that we've said our conditions
must be met by 6 p.m. on Thursday. We've said that if
they aren't, we would have to execute you.

WEST: Ah.

CARLOS: What I wanted to say to you was that we don't expect
the deadline will be met . . .

WEST: What?

CARLOS: It hardly ever is; it's just an arbitrary date we pick on,
it sometimes takes the government a long time to agree to
our terms. So you don't need to worry if nothing's happened by Thursday.

WEST: Well, I'm sure that's very thoughtful of you, but as a
matter of fact, I've no idea what day it is, and even if I did,
I couldn't see to look at my bloody watch, could I?

CARLOS: That's true, Mr. West, all I wanted was to reassure you
you're not really in any danger. We have no intention of
harming you, we, most of us, don't believe in attacking
civilians or foreign nationals, whatever interests they

represent. And the government will certainly do what we ask before they allow you to be harmed—they may not care about their people, but they tenderly love their investors. So you shouldn't worry too much. I know this is very inconvenient for you, but when we let you go, everyone will be very nice to you, and you can go back to England and sell your story to the papers for a few thousand pounds. You'll be very famous.

WEST: Well, it must be my birthday.

CARLOS: Someone will be in as soon as we can manage it to make you more comfortable and give you some food, I'm sure you must be hungry.

WEST: Why did you pick on me?

CARLOS: For poetic reasons.

WEST (*surprised*): What do you mean?

CARLOS: We liked your name.

(*He exits quietly, without* WEST *hearing.* WEST *is silent for a moment, then he does the equivalent of drawing himself up to his full height.*)

WEST: I wish to lodge a formal protest on behalf of Her Majesty's Government against this barbaric assault on a representative of the Crown, a premeditated act of violence contrary to all . . .

BLACKOUT

Four

Bare stage. The sound of rattles and a rhythmic stamping. Two INDIANS *enter, dancing, spinning and playing rattles. Behind them, three* INDIANS *carrying the funeral posts on their shoulders, circling and stamping, until, at a sign from the* CHIEF, *they 'plant' them ritually at the back of the stage in silence. In the course of the play these posts will be gradually decorated with feather head-dresses, shell belts, straw arms, etc., until they finally come to resemble the dead chiefs they represent.*

WEST *appears.*

WEST: Origin of the stars.

The children were always hungry.

Their parents said: 'We give you all we can, why do you complain?'

But the children only cried and said again that they were hungry.

In the ashes of the fire their mother found the jaw-bone of a tapir and threw it to them.

They took what meat they could from the bone and divided it among the youngest.

When they saw there was nothing left, they knew that they would have to leave.

They joined hands, sang a song and climbed slowly up into the sky.

Their mother said: 'Come back, come back. We will find more food for you. Forgive us.'

And the children answered: 'There is nothing to forgive. We know you did what you could. We bear no grudge.'

They said: 'We are better gone. Here we can help you. Here we can help to lift the darkness from you.'

And they became the stars.

(*Silence.* INDIAN GIRLS *cross to the posts and begin to paint them. The drone of a light aircraft as the* LIGHTS DIM *to* BLACKOUT.)

Five

West's house. WEST, MRS. WEST *and* MILES CRAWSHAW, *an anthropologist, sit drinking coffee after dinner.*

WEST: Well, of course, the first I heard of it was through Mrs. Hardcastle.

CRAWSHAW: Who's she?

WEST: Haven't I ever told you about Mrs. Hardcastle?

CRAWSHAW: I don't think so.

MRS. WEST (*drily*): Are you sure?

CRAWSHAW: Yes.

WEST: Mrs. Hardcastle first wrote to the Embassy, what, two or three years ago. From Bognor Regis. She said she was a widow with a little surplus cash to invest in something adventurous, and that an ad in the personal column of *The Times* offering land for sale in Brazil had caught her beady eye. So, never one to do things by halves, as she rightly remarked, she had purchased a hunk of the Mato Grosso, slightly larger, according to her computations, than West Sussex. The company to whom she had handed over her nest-egg had come through with many a bland assurance about the excellence of the roads leading to her land, which was divided equally, it seemed, between arable pasture, potential oilfields and fabulous diamond and gold-mines. Was there running water, she demanded sternly, was there . . . sanitation? Good heavens, yes, the company replied, in precisely such items as these lay the miraculous value of the transaction. So would I be so kind as to investigate for her? Need I say more? What they had sold Mrs. Hardcastle and no doubt many another hapless buffoon the length and breadth of the British Isles, the U.S.A. and the Bundesrepublik, was the most arid, inhospitable, impenetrable piece of land you could ever hope to come across. I wrote to her. All is not milk and honey, Mrs. Hardcastle, I said, and if you want to visit the land of Hardcastlia, you should start the parachute lessons right away. Well, then all hell broke loose. And because the company was so elusive, it broke all over me. The air was royal blue with the plaints of Mrs. Hardcastle. Well, when I began to get one or two other similar inquiries, I thought I'd better try to look into it a bit. What I discovered was that the land which was being sold to these hardy investors really only had one feature of any great interest—it was land which in more enlightened times had been ceded in perpetuity to various Indian tribes. Now the companies that were selling the land were of course quite well aware of this—and being men of the most scrupulous integrity and in many cases landlords themselves they knew there could be nothing more serious than to infringe the sacred laws of property. Happily, before long someone came up with an extremely simple and efficient method of protecting the Indians from land-grabbers: extermination. And so that's what was happening. They were bombing them, machine-gunning them, poisoning them, infecting them with diseases, no expense spared. None of this of course was of any interest to Mrs. Hardcastle, so I thought I wouldn't burden her with the details. I simply explained to her that though the terms of the original ad were to say the least somewhat fulsome, the company were doing what it could to improve the site. (*Pause.*) We still maintain a lively correspondence. She's not quite so incensed any more. She's done ever so much better in Nigeria.

CRAWSHAW: Did you do anything about it?

WEST: What?

CRAWSHAW: When you found out what was going on.

WEST: Well, there wasn't very much I could do. I mentioned it to a few people, you know? But I couldn't actually do anything unless what was happening was against the interests of British subjects. Which of course this wasn't. Quite the contrary. Quite the contrary. (*Pause.*) Rather more possible for someone in your line, I would have thought.

CRAWSHAW: You must be joking. Anthropologists aren't supposed to make comments on political matters, you know, in fact they're not supposed to make comments about anything very much. They're supposed to forget that the people they're working with are human and treat them as if they were an ancient monument, or a graph, or a geological formation. That's what we call science. If I'm writing a thesis about marriage practices among the Bororo, for instance, and I get fed up with writing about exogamous moieties and say as a matter of fact it doesn't make much odds who they marry because the rate things are going they'll all be dead in ten years' time anyway, I'd be told that's not anthropology, it's journalism.

WEST: I see.

CRAWSHAW: So what'll happen is, I'll finish my thesis, which will
be so boring and full of technical jargon they'll roll over
with delight, and I'll get my fellowship and start inching
my way up the hierarchy, and finally, in about thirty years'
time, I might be able to heave my weary bum on to some
decaying Chair of Anthropology. And in the meantime
some enterprising fellow with a much more practical bent
than me, and a far more modest objective will have paid a
visit to the tribe I build my reputation on, and without
paying the slightest attention to kinship structures, he'll
simply give them a couple of bags of sugar mixed with
arsenic, or a few gallons of cachaça, or a dose of measles.
And I'll be saying to my students, they had a social
structure every bit as complex as ours, when they were alive,
their way of life was perfectly adapted to their environment,
when they were alive, they were happier than we are, when
they were alive.

MRS. WEST: Oh, come on, Miles, surely it's not that bad.

CRAWSHAW: Well, it is. I sort of hate anthropologists.

WEST: I thought things were getting better now.

CRAWSHAW: What gave you that idea?

WEST: Well, ever since those revelations in when was it, '68 was
it? When all those Indian Protection Service men were put
on trial.

CRAWSHAW: Ah, yes.

(LIGHTS DOWN *on* WEST *and* MRS. WEST *and* UP *on a
government office. The* GENERAL, *in uniform and dark glasses
sits behind a large, chaste desk, its only ornament a large
granite crucifix. The* ATTORNEY GENERAL, *who wears a sober
dark suit, sits to one side, nervous.* DIM LIGHT *still on*
CRAWSHAW.)

GENERAL: Senhor, as the Minister has seen fit to release to the
press some of the details concerning the corruption of the
Indian Protection Service, we have decided to appoint you
the head of a full judicial inquiry into the matter.

ATTORNEY GENERAL: Yes, General.

GENERAL: I want you to get right to the bottom of this, Senhor,
I want the world press to see how seriously we in Brazil

35

take our responsibilities in these matters.

ATTORNEY GENERAL: Yes, General.

CRAWSHAW: Some months later.

GENERAL: Well, Senhor, how is the inquiry proceeding?

ATTORNEY GENERAL: We have had the most extraordinary results, General. We have accumulated such a vast mass of evidence, we are becoming quite desperate. For lack of space to store it, I mean. (*He laughs obsequiously.*)

GENERAL: And what are your general conclusions, Senhor?

ATTORNEY GENERAL: My general conclusions, General, are that, as you so wisely remarked, the Indian Protection Service is a sink of iniquity. Very few of them will be cleared. Apart from the cases of murder, rape and enslavement, we estimate that over the last ten years more than 62 million dollars' worth of property has been stolen from the Indians. We have 42 charges against the head of the service alone, the Major. Including the embezzlement of 300,000 dollars.

GENERAL: Excellent, well done, Senhor.

ATTORNEY GENERAL: Thank you, General, but that's not all. You see, what we've discovered is that the Indian Protection Service really plays a very insignificant part in the whole picture. They're only small fry. The people who are really responsible are far more powerful, land-speculators and landowners, a large number of Brazilian companies and even some foreign corporations . . .

GENERAL: I see.

ATTORNEY GENERAL: And furthermore . . .

GENERAL: Thank you, Senhor, that will be all. Except for one thing. I happen to know there's an empty wing at the Ministry of Agriculture, so if you're having storage problems, please have all your documents sent there, will you?

ATTORNEY GENERAL: Yes, General.

CRAWSHAW: Later still.

GENERAL: Well, Senhor, you will be pleased to hear that we have decided to dissolve and abolish the Indian Protection Service, and replace it with a new body, the Fundação

Nacional do Indio, FUNAI. This will be an entirely reconstituted and efficient organisation, under the direct jurisdiction of the army. As you know, recruitment for these arduous and, it must be admitted, not particularly well-paid posts has never been easy, but on this occasion we have been able to solve the problem by transferring a large number of men from the Indian Protection Service.

ATTORNEY GENERAL: But, General . . .

GENERAL: They have all determined to turn over a new leaf, Senhor.

ATTORNEY GENERAL: Even the Major?

GENERAL: The Colonel, Senhor, as he now is, has been transferred to the Air Ministry. The new head of FUNAI is an excellent man, a personal friend of mine. A general.

ATTORNEY GENERAL: But, General, what about all the evidence we have collected?

GENERAL: Ah, yes Senhor, I forgot to tell you. By some curious quirk of fate, there was a disastrous fire last night at the Ministry of Agriculture. The west wing was, alas, completely destroyed.

ATTORNEY GENERAL: But, General, what am I going to say to the Minister?

GENERAL: Senhor, for some reason best known to himself, the Minister has seen fit to hand in his resignation. Now, if you'd be good enough to excuse me, I'm expecting a call from the American Embassy. Good morning.

(LIGHTS DOWN *on* GENERAL *and* ATTORNEY GENERAL *and* UP *on* WEST *and* MRS. WEST. *Silence.* CRAWSHAW *sits, smiling.*)

WEST (*smiling*): I'm sure it didn't quite happen like that.

CRAWSHAW (*his smile disappearing*): More or less. What's the difference how it happened?

WEST: No, I . . . suppose you're right. (*Pause.*) Would you like a brandy or something?

CRAWSHAW (*nodding*): Thanks.

WEST: What about you, dear?

MRS. WEST: No, thanks.

(*To* CRAWSHAW, *as* WEST *moves over to the sideboard, and pours out two glasses of brandy.*)

It keeps me awake.

CRAWSHAW *turning away from her to speak to* WEST): No, the thing is, a lot of good, young, idealistic people are going into FUNAI, but they can't do anything. They've got no resources, they don't get paid for months on end, their wives leave them, they catch malaria, everything is controlled by the army. All they can do is try to follow the government line, which is don't exterminate, integrate.

WEST: Well, at least that sounds like some kind of an improvement.

CRAWSHAW: No, no, it's the same thing, only slower.

MRS. WEST: Surely they've got to be integrated sooner or later, they can't just go on living in the Stone Age.

CRAWSHAW: That's it, you see, integration is such a friendly word, no one ever remembers that if people do get integrated, they get integrated into the bottom layer, which in Brazil means they get integrated into the urban proletariat, who are overcrowded, under-employed and desperate, or into the peasantry, who in large areas of the country are simply starving. Integrate them, give them the benefits of civilisation, the government says. What they don't say is that the first two benefits of civilisation the Indians are going to be given are disease and alcohol. All they mean when they say the Indians have got to be integrated is that the Indians have got to give up their land and a totally self-sufficient and harmonious way of life to become the slaves of slaves.

WEST: Well, that may be what happens, Miles, but I'm sure it's not the government's intention.

CRAWSHAW: What about BR–80, then?

MRS. WEST: What's that?

WEST: The road.

CRAWSHAW: The Transamazon Highway. Look, almost the only place in Brazil where the Indians are protected, looked after and allowed to lead their own lives is the Xingu Indian Park. The road was planned to pass north of the park. Now they've decided, at great inconvenience and expense, to move it, so it goes bang through the middle. Why do you think they've done that?

WEST: Didn't they offer a new grant of land to make up for it?

CRAWSHAW: None of that land to the south can support life. They just want to get rid of the Park. It's no secret, they keep saying they want to get rid of it in their speeches. Listen, just the other day, the head of FUNAI, the Minister of Indian Affairs, said: 'We must remove these ethnic cysts from the face of Brazil.' That's what I call putting your cards on the table.

WEST: Well, I don't know nearly as much about it as you do. As I say, I just got to hear about it in a roundabout way via Mrs. Hardcastle. What I'm really interested in is their legends.

CRAWSHAW: Legends?

WEST: Yes, I publish, I mean I have had published, a few what we used to call slim volumes of verse, um, poetry, you know. Nothing very grand, just a small independent publisher . . .

MRS. WEST (*drily*): Thrust Press.

WEST: Yes, and I want to do a collection, I mean I got very interested, and they seemed to me very beautiful, some of them, of Indian legends. You know, so I've been trying to collect them.

CRAWSHAW: I see.

WEST (*laughing nervously*): You seem a bit dubious.

CRAWSHAW: Well, I suppose I am, really. I don't really approve of the idea of presenting the Indian myths on their own like a lot of pretty children's stories, without trying to show that they're just an aspect of an extremely complex and sophisticated society. It's the kind of thing that reinforces people's prejudice.

WEST: Well, I've approached them . . . I mean, to me they're just like er, Greek legends, or . . . something like that.

CRAWSHAW: I'm sorry, it's very rude of me to judge them, without even having read them, I just . . .

WEST: Well, I'll er . . .

(*Brief silence. Then* CRAWSHAW *rises abruptly.*)

CRAWSHAW: Excuse me a minute.

(*He exits swiftly. A moment's silence.*)

MRS. WEST: He's not a bit like James, is he?

WEST: No, well, I shouldn't think our children would be anything like us. If we had any.

MRS. WEST: What's that supposed to mean?

WEST: Nothing. (*He crosses to the sideboard, pours himself another brandy.*)

MRS. WEST: He wasn't very nice about your poetry, was he?

WEST: You're not very nice about my poetry.

MRS. WEST: I've never said anything about your poetry.

WEST: Exactly.

(*Silence.* WEST *sips his brandy.*)

MRS. WEST: You know something, we're going to have to get rid of Maria.

WEST: Why?

MRS. WEST: The dinner was disgusting. I've told her how to make rice pudding, I've explained it to her time and again; tonight it was so cold and full of lumps it was more like school porridge.

WEST: I can't sack her for not being able to make rice pudding.

MRS. WEST: Why not, that's what she's paid for, isn't it, you pay her enough.

WEST: I pay her next to nothing.

MRS. WEST: Well, it's a lot to them.

(WEST *sighs. Silence.* CRAWSHAW *returns, sits.*)

CRAWSHAW: When I was in the lavatory just now, I thought of something that happened the other evening. I was at a dinner-party and there was a woman there who told a story she could hardly get out for laughing. Apparently she has an Indian servant, very unsophisticated, practically a savage, I think she said, but very good-natured and very willing. Anyhow, one day she'd asked him to put a new roll of lavatory paper in one of her bathrooms. An hour or so later, she wanted him for something else, but at first she couldn't find him. Eventually she discovered him in the bathroom. He was winding the new roll of lavatory paper very slowly and very carefully on to the core of the used roll. He just couldn't work out how else to do it, she said, and by this time she was laughing so hard I thought her teeth were going to drop out. He looked so funny, she said, hooting and spluttering, you can't imagine, bent over concentrating with his tongue sticking out. (*He shakes his head.*) Extraordinary story, I thought. Everyone else seemed to think it was hilarious.

(*Silence.* MRS. WEST *laughs abruptly.*)

MRS. WEST: Well, you must admit it is quite funny, isn't it?

BLACKOUT

Six

The guerrilla hideout. WEST *no longer wears a hood and is handcuffed by his left hand to the bedpost with what seems to be a home-made handcuff designed to give him maximum flexibility. He is lying in the most comfortable position available to him, staring blankly out into space. The door opens and* CARLOS *enters.* WEST *takes a brief glance at him, then jerks his head violently away towards the side wall.*

CARLOS: It's all right, Mr. West, you needn't worry.

(WEST *turns back slowly, looks at* CARLOS.)

WEST: What?

CARLOS: Doesn't matter now if you see me. My executive has decided that I am to accompany our comrades to Cuba and carry on my work there.

WEST: So you're the bastard.

CARLOS: What? (*He grins broadly.*) Oh, yes, I'm the bastard.

WEST: I won't forget you.

CARLOS: Well, I'm sure I won't forget you.

WEST: Why are they sending you to Cuba, aren't you good enough?

CARLOS: This is none of your business, Mr. West. (*Pause.*) I came to tell you that we are making some progress in our negotiations with the dictatorship.

WEST: Oh?

CARLOS: Yes. Things haven't been going as smoothly this time as in the past, but it looks as if it's going to be all right now.

41

We hope to have you out of here in a week or so.

WEST: I'm glad to hear it.

CARLOS (*smiling*): Patience.

(*Silence.*)

WEST: Look, I know it's no good my saying this, but I really don't think this is the right way to go about things, you know. I mean, I realise everything's very bad for you at the moment, but this kind of thing isn't going to get you anywhere. It just puts um people's backs up. What I mean is, if you leave it alone for a while, I'm sure things will improve in the future.

CARLOS: The future is the only kind of property that the masters willingly concede to their slaves. Camus.

WEST: I see.

(*Silence.*)

CARLOS: I wanted to ask if there was anything you wanted, any way we could make you more comfortable.

WEST: Well. (*He reflects a moment.*) I was wondering if you could find something a bit lighter for me to read. (*He indicates a pile of books on a table by the bed.*) I mean, it's all very interesting, all this stuff you've left me, and not the sort of thing I'd normally have happened across, but I do find it, you know, all those statistics and so on, rather tiring.

CARLOS: I'll ask around the boys, see what we can dig up.

WEST: Thanks. Oh, and there is just one other thing.

CARLOS: What?

WEST: Can you let me have a pen and some paper?

CARLOS (*hesitating*): What for?

WEST: Well, I write poetry, you know, in fact I've had some published. What we used to call slim volumes of verse.

CARLOS (*dubiously*): Oh, I see.

WEST: In fact when you said you'd kidnapped me for poetic reasons, I thought for a moment it was because you'd taken against my work. I thought, very erudite class of kidnappers they have nowadays.

(*He laughs nervously.* CARLOS *is frowning, not listening.*)

CARLOS: Well, I suppose that's all right.

WEST (*pleased*): Oh.

42

CARLOS: But you must write in Portuguese.

WEST: Portuguese?

CARLOS: Yes, well, you can't expect us to let you write in English, can you? As far as the others are concerned, you could be writing anything. Anyway, your Portuguese is very good, it'll be good exercise for you, interesting for us.

WEST: All right, then.

(CARLOS *moves over towards the door. As he does so,* WEST *suddenly jerks upright, his expression ferocious.*)

You're never going to get away with this, you know.

(CARLOS *startled, stops. Then bursts out laughing.*)

CARLOS: Oh, come on.

WEST (*hurt*): Well.

CARLOS: You play chess?

WEST: Erm, yes, why?

CARLOS: Well?

WEST: I enjoy it.

CARLOS: O.K., we must play. I'm very good. (*Pause.*) Maybe we aren't going to get away with it, but it doesn't matter. There are plenty of others to carry on with the work. They try very hard, but: no-one can blot out the sun with one finger. Carlos Marighela.

(*Silence.* WEST *raises his handcuffed wrist.*)

WEST: Man is born free, but is everywhere in chains. Rousseau.

(CARLOS *laughs and exits.* WEST *alone, smiling.*)

BLACKOUT

Seven

An office. A desk, covered with papers and books, some of them pushed aside to make way for a tape-recorder. Behind the desk, an American INVESTIGATOR. *Sitting at an angle, facing the microphone nervously,* ATAIDE PEREIRA, *wearing a check shirt and baggy trousers. In his lap a sweat-stained hat.*

INVESTIGATOR: Move a little closer.

    (PEREIRA *does so.*)

               Now you know what you're saying here is on your honour.

               Just as if you were in court under oath.

PEREIRA: Yes sir.

      Yes I do.

    (*The* INVESTIGATOR *switches on the tape-recorder.*)

INVESTIGATOR: How did you come to be involved in all this
               In the first place?

PEREIRA: Well.

      Even after the bombing they were still causing some trouble.

      So the Company asked Senhor de Brito to hire some men for an expedition

      And I was one of them.

INVESTIGATOR: How did you feel about the mission?

PEREIRA: O.K.

      I felt fine.

      Look at it this way.

      Those Indians are on valuable land

      Sitting there doing nothing

      And sometimes they can be hostile.

      There's no way you can move them out

      So what else can you do?

      To be honest I was quite looking forward to it.

      Made a change.

      And then there was the money of course.

      I know it probably seems wrong to you

      But to us it's just like going hunting.

      You see we're taught to think of them as animals.

      At least that's what the boss always calls them.

      Animals.

      He asked us to bring back a couple for him.

      He likes to take them for what he calls

      The trip to the dentist.

      Open wide he says.

      Say aah he says.

Then he puts his pistol in their mouth
And blows their brains out. (*Pause.*)
Myself I'm a very good shot.
That's why I was chosen.

INVESTIGATOR: How many of you were there?

PEREIRA: Six.
Including Chico.
He was the leader.
That was the one thing we weren't too happy about.
Because Chico well
He'd cut your head off soon as say good morning.

INVESTIGATOR: Tell me about the expedition.

PEREIRA: Well it was no picnic
I can tell you that.
First of all we travelled upstream for a few days.
Then we left the launch and set off into the jungle.
Chico had a compass
Japanese it was.
Didn't stop us getting lost.
We were wandering around for days
And by the time we found somewhere we recognised
We'd run out of food.
Luckily before too long the plane came over
And dropped us some more.
But it wasn't all that long
Before that ran out as well.
Eventually we found a village.

INVESTIGATOR: What happened then?

PEREIRA: Well nothing really.
Somebody'd beaten us to it.
Nothing but corpses all over the place
And a terrible stench.
Still we did get some food there
Dug up some manioc
That kind of thing.
Then we pressed on.
By this time we were all pretty jumpy.
For one thing we were in diamond country

45

And you know what they're like
Shoot and no questions asked.
Also the rains had started
So every day we got drenched
And the insects that were just hatching out
Ate us alive.
Chico was in a really filthy mood.
So were we all.

INVESTIGATOR: Go on.

PEREIRA: We knew we were warm
So we were very careful very strict
No talking
No smoking
Keeping several yards apart.
And finally
After all that time
One evening
We saw their village through the trees.

BLACKOUT

Eight

Ancient, scratchy 78 r.p.m. recording of Gilbert & Sullivan—
'Selections from The Pirates of Penzance' *or something like that.*
WEST *sits, sipping a tall drink, on the veranda of a modest colonial*
bungalow, with its owner, MAJOR BRIGG, *a leathery old party, dressed*
in khaki shirt, shorts, long socks with a ribbon, in fact everything but
the topee. Sundown.

BRIGG: Well, nice to have some company for once.

WEST: Yes.

BRIGG: Always enjoy this time of day the best, you know.
Sitting down, bit of a drink. Doesn't last long, of course,
it'll be pitch black before you know where you are. My wife
always used to get furious, time for your drink, she'd say,

46

and I'd say, just finishing up one or two things, be with you in a tick, and of course by the time I got out it was like the middle of the night and we'd both be in a temper all evening. (*Pause.*) D'you think I should go back home?

WEST: To England?

BRIGG: Yes.

WEST: Well, I don't know, I think you'd find it very different . . .

BRIGG: Oh, yes, I know that. Time of the General Strike I left, you know. Always like to think that was deliberate but actually it was a complete coincidence. Of course, I was there for some of the war, and I've been on leave a few times, but you don't get much impression. Don't suppose I could afford it, anyway.

WEST: It has got very expensive.

BRIGG: Yes, and I never paid any of those stamp things, so I wouldn't get a proper pension. Can't think why I want to go back really, just a sort of an urge. (*Pause. The record has ended.* BRIGG *gets up.*) D'you like Gilbert and Sullivan?

WEST: Erm . . . I really don't know that much about them.

BRIGG: Remarkable pair. (*He crosses to the gramophone, winds it up and turns the record over.*) Damn difficult to get hold of the needles for this thing.

(*He looks expectantly at* WEST, *who, though embarrassed, refuses to take the hint.*)

WEST: Yes, I'm sure.

(*Silence.* BRIGG *sits down again and the music crackles out.*)

BRIGG: You mustn't think it's something new, you know, all this you've been telling me. They've been killing them off ever since I can remember and before, in fact, good God, they were killing off the poor beggars in Shakespeare's day. It's nothing new. But at least when I went into the Indian Protection Service, we actually did make some sort of a stab at protecting them. Now, as far as I can gather, it's the I.P.S. you go to if you want them done away with.

WEST: There certainly has been a great deal of corruption . . .

BRIGG: Corruption? It may be. It may be they've just given up in despair. I did. You don't have the money, you don't have the equipment, you don't have the authority. At least when

47

I joined the Service, after the war, you knew more or less what you were up against and you could do something about it. But by the time I left the whole thing had become so industrialised and so efficient, there was absolutely nothing to be done. And I suppose they all feel, well, if you can't beat 'em, join 'em.

WEST: What exactly do you mean, industrialised?

BRIGG: I can remember, in about '47 I suppose it would have been, sitting up a tree on the Aripuanã, because we knew these fellers were trying to get rid of some Indians so that they could get at some diamonds or some damn thing or another. Anyway, sure enough, I hadn't been there very long, when these two chaps appeared in a boat. In those days the favoured approach was to get blankets from the smallpox ward of a hospital and distribute them, you see, among the Indians—that way, with a bit of luck, you could polish off the whole tribe. And, needless to say, the boat was full of blankets. So I shouted to them and told them to stand and deliver, as it were.

WEST: And did they?

BRIGG: No, they didn't take a blind bit of notice.

WEST: So what did you do?

BRIGG: Well, I shot them.

WEST: Ah.

BRIGG: Shot 'em dead. Oh, yes, You see, that's what I mean, in those days there was something you could do about it, you could take some direct action. But nowadays, when they use bombs and machine-guns and I don't know what else, you could sit up a tree on the Aripuanã till you rotted, for all the good you could do. Ready for another?

WEST (*sipping at his still half-full glass*): In a minute.

BRIGG: Good, good.

(*Silence.*)

WEST: You must have seen some extraordinary things in your time.

BRIGG: Yes. (*Pause.*) You know the strangest thing I ever saw?

WEST: No, what?

BRIGG: I found this body in the jungle, least it was more or less of a skeleton by the time I came across it. All his equipment and his knife and so on had been stolen, but he'd obviously been English or at any rate English-speaking.

WEST: How do you know?

BRIGG: Well, this was the thing. He'd carved this message on a huge jatoba trunk, before he died. It said IMAGINEUS, all one word, IMAGINEUS. And underneath, a sort of a map.

WEST: Good heavens, what did you do?

BRIGG: Well, nothing. I certainly wasn't going to take any notice of the map, that's always the first step to disaster, look what happened to poor old Fawcett. But the message was so intriguing, don't you think, imagine us. What could he possibly have meant, it haunted me for years.

WEST: Did you ever think of a likely explanation?

BRIGG: Well, I did, yes. In the end I decided his spelling wasn't very hot, and that what he'd actually been trying to say, in a spirit of bitter irony, was, 'I'm a genius.'
(WEST *laughs, and* BRIGG *looks at him sharply, then smiles.*)
Ready for another?

WEST: Yes, thanks.
(BRIGG *claps his hands loudly above his head. A moment later, an elderly* INDIAN *in an ill-fitting white suit appears, takes the glasses and shuffles back into the bungalow.*)

BRIGG: I told you he was the last surviving member of his tribe, didn't I?

WEST: Yes. What did you say his name was?

BRIGG: Oh, I don't know, he has some endless unpronounceable name, but I call him Bert, after my late brother. The rest of the tribe all died of a 'flu epidemic, you know. Caught it off me. One of our many failures. He's been with me about twenty years, and I suppose he's the real reason I don't go back home.

WEST: I wonder if he'd remember any of his tribe's legends. I think I told you I'm rather interested in collecting legends.
(*The* INDIAN *reappears with the drinks.*)

BRIGG: Oh, it's no good asking him anything like that, I'm afraid he hasn't got much between the ears, poor old beggar.

(*The* INDIAN *exits. Silence.*)

I must say, it's nice to have a bit of company. (*Pause.*) You know, one thing I never could get used to all those years was them not wearing any clothes. I know it's silly, but I never could get used to it. Bloody heathen habit, if you ask me.

WEST: Oh, I don't know about that.

BRIGG (*vehemently*): There's no hope for them, you know. No hope. Not a chance. Might as well be philosophical about it. I sometimes think the best thing is for them to get it all over with as quickly as possible. Let's have a record. (*He gets up and puts on another record, this time some gay number of the twenties. He sits down again.*) Cheers.

WEST: Cheers.

(*Silence except for the oppressively jolly record.*)

BRIGG: Quite good some of this modern stuff.

(*Silence.*)

WEST (*pensive*): Imagine us.

BLACKOUT

Nine

WEST: Origin of music.
> One evening a strange boy arrived in our village.
> He told us he came from the house of the sun.
> He said he was here to bring us a great gift.
> Then he sang for us and we felt for the first time
> The beauty of music.

> But before very long our men began to die
> And we found that those who came back from the river
>   ate their fish and listened to his song
> Died in the night.

So we explained to the boy that we would have to kill him
And he asked to be burnt.

As he died in the flames he sang his most beautiful song
And from his ashes grew the paxiuba palm.
Now our men make their flutes from its wood.
And sometimes in the evening we have music
Strange and beautiful as the boy from the house of the sun
And sad as his dying.

(*Flute solo. The* INDIANS *continue decorating the funeral
posts.*)

BLACKOUT

Ten

The guerrilla hideout. WEST, *still handcuffed, has been playing chess
with* CARLOS. *Now he contemplates the board, shrugs, makes a
gesture with his free hand and pushes over his king. He looks up at*
CARLOS, *smiling and shaking his head.*

CARLOS: Told you I was good.

WEST: Yes. You are quite.

    (CARLOS *smiles, executes a courtly bow, gets up and moves
    round the room, stretching.*)

CARLOS: Want another game?

WEST: Oh, not just now, I don't think. Later on perhaps.

CARLOS: You very bored?

WEST: Yes, I suppose you might say so, yes.

CARLOS (*abstractedly*): Things move slowly. I get very bored as
    well.

WEST: I hope you don't expect me to sympathize.

CARLOS (*smiling*): No.

    (*Silence.*)

WEST: Tell me, what's your position, I mean, I didn't see
    anything about it in any of that stuff you gave me to read,

what's your policy as far as the Indians are concerned?

CARLOS: Indians?

WEST: Yes.

CARLOS: What Indians?

WEST: The Brazilian Indians.

CARLOS: Oh. Well, I suppose our policy is to protect them from exploitation just as we intend to protect the workers and the peasants.

WEST: It's not so much that they're being exploited, it's that they're being killed.

CARLOS: Oh, yes, well, I know about that, of course. It's just one of the things we'd have to put a stop to, isn't it?

WEST: Not so easy.

CARLOS: No, probably not, but then neither are a lot of things. I must say, compared with most of the difficulties we'd have to face, it is rather a marginal problem. Why do you ask?

WEST: I'm just interested in them, that's all, I know quite a lot about them.

CARLOS: Well, so do we.

WEST: Mm.

(*Silence.*)

CARLOS: You write some poems?

WEST: No.

CARLOS: Oh, I'm sorry, why not? I was looking forward to seeing them.

WEST: Well, I don't know, I haven't been feeling at my best for one reason or another. (*He indicates the handcuff.*) Also I'm left-handed.

CARLOS (*seriously*): Oh, yes, well, that does make things difficult, I can see. (*Brightening.*) You can dictate them to me, if you like.

WEST: Also I do find the idea of writing in Portuguese rather . . . inhibiting.

CARLOS: Well, sketch them out in English if you want to, then translate them into Portuguese, then give us the English so we can destroy it, you keep the Portuguese and translate it back when you get out.

WEST: I'll see.

CARLOS: Listen, I wrote a poem yesterday, I'm going to read it
to you, then when you write your poems you can read
them to me and we can discuss them, it'll be interesting.
All right? (*He produces a piece of paper from his inside pocket.*)
WEST: All right.
CARLOS: It's called 'The New Beatitudes'. (*He considers his piece
of paper a moment.*) 'The New Beatitudes.'
Blessed are the corporations: for theirs are the kingdoms of
the world.
Blessed are the complacent: for they shall never mourn.
Blessed are the aggressive: for they have inherited the earth.
Blessed are they which do hunger and thirst after nothing
but righteousness: for they shall be easily satisfied.
Blessed are the merciless: for they shall obtain power.
Blessed are the pure in race: for they shall see themselves
as God.
Blessed are the armed forces: for they shall call themselves
the children of the Revolution.
Blessed are they which persecute others for righteousness'
sake: for theirs are the kingdoms of the world.
Blessed are ye when men shall revile you and say all manner
of evil against you for the sake of the poor and starving.
Send for the censor and secret police.
Rejoice and be exceeding glad.
Smear the electrodes and sharpen the knives.
Ye own the salt of the earth: but if the salt have lost his
market value, invest in real estate.
(*He thrusts the piece of paper back into his inside pocket, looks
expectantly at* WEST.)
WEST: Erm . . .
CARLOS: Like it?
WEST (*hesitantly*): Yes. I mean, it's a little bit more direct and er
crude than what I'm used to.
CARLOS: Yes, well, you see, we haven't time for all your old
European bourgeois subtleties.
WEST: I don't know if that's quite . . .
CARLOS: Myself, I think if anything it's too literary, not direct
enough.

WEST: Well . . .

CARLOS: The understanding of a poem should be not merely an intellectual advance, but a political advance. Fanon. And he also said the national culture of an underdeveloped country should take its place at the very heart of the struggle for freedom. He said that in the revolutionary phase many people who under normal circumstances would never have dreamt of producing literary work have a job to do—as awakeners of the people.

WEST: I suppose it depends what . . .

CARLOS: You see what interesting discussions we can have.
(*Silence.*)

WEST: Your people are against organised religion, are you?

CARLOS: No, not particularly. Why do you ask?

WEST: Well, the poem . . .

CARLOS: Oh, no, that's . . . No, many of the priests in Brazil, and especially the young ones, are with us, which is very good for us, because they know how to speak to the people. Of course, there are plenty of the other sort and nowadays they're importing them from Spain, because they're so clever at explaining how dictators are the beloved of God and how the poor are the only ones who'll be admitted to heaven, except, of course, for those members of the ruling class who've kept up their subscriptions.

WEST: Do they tell them to turn the other cheek?

CARLOS: Yes, yes, repeatedly. Are you a religious man, Mr. West?

WEST: Not at all.

CARLOS: Good, good. Let me see if I can get you a drink.
(BLACKOUT *as he strides towards the door, beaming.*)

Eleven

The main room of the Revd. Elmer Penn's spotlessly clean bungalow. Everything is extremely tidy and strictly functional. Among the more prominent objects, a desk, filing cabinets, a deep-freeze unit and a harmonium. PENN *enters, followed by* WEST, *who looks somewhat grim and strained. Hum of an air-conditioner.*

PENN: Well, now, that's pleasant, isn't it? I don't know what we'd do out here without air-conditioning. I expect you'd like something to drink. (*He moves over and flips up the lid of the deep-freeze unit.*)
(WEST *brightens visibly.*)
I'm afraid we don't keep any alcohol in the mission; since we don't allow the Indians to partake of any, we feel we have to ask our visitors to forgo it as well. We have Coke, 7-up, all kindsa soft drinks. (*He helps himself to a Coca-Cola, which he opens with a device on the side of the deep-freeze unit, takes a straw and turns to look inquiringly at* WEST.)

WEST: Er, no thanks, I won't.

PENN: No? (*He closes the deep-freeze unit, moves over and sits in the chair by the desk, indicating the more comfortable armchair to* WEST.) Sit down.
(WEST *does so.*)
Well? What do you think?

WEST (*uneasily*): It's . . . very impressive.

PENN: Glad you think so. Tell you the truth, we're very proud of it ourselves. It's not been an easy job, I can tell you. Five years it's taken to get to this stage, five years. And there's been numberless times I've wanted to give the whole thing up and go home. Numberless times. But I always used to say to myself, forgive me, Alan, but I really did used to say it, Moses laboured forty years as a shepherd, and our Lord Himself spent many years sawing lumber in a carpenter's shop. And that used to help some. But as I say, we've had our problems.
(*Brief silence.*)

WEST: Why . . . why have you put, got barbed wire round the village?

PENN: Well, Alan, I've been expecting you to ask about that, I could see you were surprised when you arrived, many of our visitors are. Believe me, it's for their own protection. You see, we felt when we arrived, and you must understand that when Maybelle and I arrived here five years ago, it was so

55

primitive, it was like something out of the pages of the *National Geographic Magazine*—we felt that what was very important was to make a clear distinction, clear enough to be unmistakable to the Indians, between what they had in the past and what we were offering them for the future. Well, now, after the first steps, when the only thing you really need is a little courage and frankly nerve, and believe me, if there's one thing even a Stone Age savage can understand, it's raw courage—you consolidate. Now when I say consolidate, that probably sounds quite easy to you, but what it really involves is more than three years of very very hard work, in which you have to learn their language, teach them the Gospel in terms they can understand, show them that your medicine is better and more effective than the shaman's, win them away from their own primitive beliefs and, well, I suppose one has to be honest about this, make them dependent on you. Well, when you have achieved all that, there comes a moment, and I suppose judging that moment correctly is the most difficult job we have in the civilisation process, there comes a moment when you have to move from the defensive to the offensive. And when that moment comes, you have to say to the Indian, look, either you must go forward with us, or you must leave the flock. You see, for a long time the new concepts you've introduced them to co-exist with a lot of the bad old ways and there just has to be a confrontation, when you say to them, if you don't want to renounce the stimulants and intoxicants that are preventing you from becoming a useful member of the community, if you don't want to accept what we do for you, why you're just going to have to go your own way. It's a very delicate task and it's really impossible to avoid stepping on a few cultural toes, but if as I say you choose the moment carefully, you'll only lose a very small number of them. And of the rest you can truly say:

> The race that long in darkness pined
> Have seen a glorious light.

WEST: And the wire?

PENN: Is to protect them from outside influence during this very critical period. I don't want you to think they're not free to come and go. Anybody can join the community providing he understands its rules and agrees to abide by them, and of course if anyone has a reason for wanting to leave the village for a few days, all he has to do is come and see me and I make the necessary arrangements. Hopefully it won't be too long before the stabilisation phase is completed and then we'll be able to dismantle the wire—and I might be able to think about having myself a little vacation. (*He laughs heartily, then adds.*) The Indians put the wire up themselves, you know.

WEST: Really?

PENN: Oh, yes, sure they did. You see, Alan, alongside of preaching the Gospel, which is of course our primary task, there are other ways in which we have to change the lives of these savages. For instance, we have to instil in them a work ethic tied to a reward system, which is something quite new to them. Now, if you do that, naturally they're going to have to look at a whole lot of things in a new way, things like property and personal possessions, and they're going to want to preserve and protect them.

WEST: I see.

PENN: People have these very romantic ideas about the Indians. Give you an example, this thing about clothes, people always say the Indian doesn't like clothes, doesn't want clothes, he's proud to go naked. It's just not true. You should have seen the fighting and the quarrelling when we issued them with T-shirts. Course they had no idea how to put them on, it's one of the funniest sights I ever seen, all of them struggling with those things, you know, trying to put their heads through the armholes, my, we did laugh.

WEST: But, Mr. Penn . . .

PENN: Elmer, Elmer.

WEST: Elmer, do you think it's a good thing, I mean, fair to them, to change their way of life so radically?

PENN: We have no choice, Alan. See, even if you leave aside the religious aspect of our work, these men have to be integrated into society, we have to bring them into our world,

57

Alan, yours and mine. Otherwise they can never survive. I
don't have to tell you there've been a lot of regrettable
incidents in the last few years because the Indians have no
understanding of the world as it is. The government knows
that—that's why they're pursuing a policy of integration.
You know, when I first came to Latin America in the forties,
they wouldn't allow foreign missionaries into Brazil at all:
thank heavens this government sees it differently and
understands the value of what we're doing, so they couldn't
be more helpful. For instance, just recently, they took
around eighty Indians into Belo Horizonte and turned them
into a crack police force. And what people don't understand
is that the Indian wants this, he sincerely wants progress.

WEST: Even if it means losing his land?

PENN: Alan, there are ninety million people in this country, you
can't expect them not to exploit its natural resources, how
else are they going to make this into a prosperous country?
They must have access to the land.

WEST: It's a pity a few of the big landowners don't know about
that.

PENN: Well, Alan, I'm not going to talk politics with you. All I
know is that this government may have some terrible
problems as of now, but it's working very closely with the
United States government, and I think together we're going
to be able to lick most of them.
(*Silence.*)

WEST: Perhaps I will have a Coca-Cola.

PENN: Sure, sure. (*He organises this, hands* WEST *an open bottle
and straw.*) A man must do what a man can do. (*Long
pause. He consults his watch.*) My goodness, it's time for
choir practice already.

WEST (*making to get up*): Oh, well, I'll . . .

PENN: No, no, I want you to see this, Alan. (*He moves to the
desk, presses a button. Chimes of an electric church-bell.*) I'm
planning a little surprise for Maybelle, when she gets back
from the States. You'll see what I mean in a minute. You're
going to meet Kumai, you know, the one I was telling you
about?

58

WEST: Oh, yes, yes, good.

PENN: He's a remarkably intelligent boy for an Indian. He's very quick-witted and kind of artistic, something of a rascal but very lovable. I've even been able to teach him a few words of English. We had a little bit of trouble with him a year or so back, but we got over that in the end.

WEST: What sort of trouble?

PENN: Well, Alan, alongside of all the other problems I was telling you about, one of the most difficult things for the savage to understand, and of course one of the things he must be made to understand, is the question of morals, I mean sexual morality. Now before we came, the custom was that a man would have a wife, but he'd also have a number of mistresses, in fact the whole tribe was extremely promiscuous, and quite openly so. Well, we made ourselves very very clear on that point and put a stop to it as far as we could. Then, after a time, Kumai came to me and told me he wanted to get married. Well, I thought the girl was rather unsuitable for him; frankly she was rather a stupid girl, but he insisted and so I agreed to marry them. Everything went along O.K. for a time, and then I noticed that his attitude toward us seemed to have changed, he became sullen and unfriendly, and looked kind of guilty all the time. Well, I looked into it, and sure enough I discovered he was paying less and less attention to his wife and had become involved with a girl who had given us nothing but trouble from the day we arrived. We weren't sure what to do, we thought about it and thought about it, and finally we realised we had to discipline him, we had no choice. What made it even harder was that Kumai understood as well, he knew he'd done wrong, and it darn near broke our hearts the way he accepted his punishment.

WEST: What was it?

PENN: We sent the two of them away. He came back a few months later. He looked terrible. Begged me to let him come back to stay. Well, of course, it was a very great joy to forgive him and accept him back into the flock.

WEST: And what happened to her?

PENN: I didn't ask him. As far as I was concerned, he'd been forgiven and the incident was closed. I've certainly never referred to it again. (*Pause.*) They should be here by now. You know, some of my more old-fashioned colleagues won't allow the Indians to even set foot in their personal quarters. I think that's very narrow-minded, don't you? The way I look at it, how are you going to win a man's confidence if you won't even let him see inside your home?

(*A tentative knock on the door.* PENN *strides over to it and lets in half a dozen* INDIANS. *By contrast with the Indians as they appear in the other scenes, these seem cowed and dejected, miserable in shabby, holed T-shirts and tatty shorts. Their manner is painfully timid and ingratiating.* PENN *grabs one of them and drags him over towards* WEST. *The others cluster over by the harmonium.*)

This is Kumai. O senhor é inglês, Kumai.

WEST: Hello, Kumai.

PENN: Have you some little thing you could give them?

WEST: Er . . . (*He searches in his pockets a moment, comes out with a handful of small change.*) How about this?

PENN: Yeah, that's O.K.

(*He takes the money, gives some to* KUMAI, *then distributes the rest carefully among the other* INDIANS.)

KUMAI: Ingiss.

WEST: Erm . . .

KUMAI: Ingiss.

WEST: Yes, that's right, English.

KUMAI: Sooba.

WEST: What?

KUMAI: Sooba. (*He makes vigorous kicking movements.*)

WEST: I . . .

PENN: He means football. They can't manage fs, you know.

WEST: Oh, football!

KUMAI (*nodding and smiling, delighted*): Sooba . . . Nobistai.

WEST: What?

KUMAI: Nobistai.

WEST: I don't . . .

PENN: Well, neither do I. What are you trying to say, Kumai?

KUMAI: Nobistai . . . Ingiss.

WEST: Oh, I see!

PENN: What?

WEST: Nobby Stiles. He's trying to say Nobby Stiles.

KUMAI (*nodding proudly*): Nobistai.

PENN: I still don't understand.

WEST (*muttering*): He's an English footballer.

PENN: Oh! (*He roars with laughter.*) Well, I'll be! He's a pack of surprises! I wonder where he could have picked that up. (*He laughs again, shaking his head.*) O.K., Kumai, let's go. (*He shepherds* KUMAI *over to the harmonium, sits him down at it. Meanwhile* WEST, *who is extremely upset, passes his hand unnoticed across his eyes.*)

WEST: Oh, my God.

(PENN *gestures to* KUMAI, *who starts to play.*)

PENN (*singing lustily*): The day . . . (*He breaks off.*) No, no, wait a minute. Again.

(*He gestures again.* KUMAI *begins again and* PENN *booms out the hymn, the* INDIANS *joining in with vaguely approximate noises.*)

(*singing*): The day thou gavest, Lord, is ended,
The darkness falls at thy behest;
To thee our morning hymns ascended,
Thy praise shall sanctify our rest.

The sun that bids us rest is waking
Our brethren 'neath the western sky,
And hour by hour fresh lips are making
Thy wondrous doings heard on high.

So be it, Lord; thy throne shall never,
Like earth's proud empires, pass away;
Thy kingdom stands, and grows for ever,
Till all thy creatures own thy sway.

(WEST, *appalled, pulls disconsolately at his Coca-Cola.*
BLACKOUT.)

INTERVAL

Twelve

The curtain rises on the long, melancholy cries which summon the Champion wrestlers of the visiting tribes to start the wrestling tournament. By now the funeral posts are fully decorated and the INDIANS *themselves ceremonially painted. An* INDIAN *enters, circles the stage warily, acknowledges the* CHIEF *and gestures to his chosen opponent, who steps forward. They circle each other, drop to their knees, slap their right hands together and engage. The wrestling match is intense but graceful, and lasts until one of the wrestlers succeeds in touching the back of his opponent's thigh, after which they embrace and move to the back of the stage, arm in arm, while the* CHIEF *summons another pair to take their place. At the end of the second wrestling match, the* CHIEF *congratulates both wrestlers and the* MEN *move into a tight group, discussing the contests and passing a gourd from one to the other.*

 WEST *appears.*

WEST: The coming of Death.

   The creator wished his children to be immortal.

   He told them to wait by the river.

   'Wait for the third canoe,' he said.

   'For in the first canoe or in the second canoe

   Will be Death.'

   After a time the first canoe passed.

   In it a basket of rotten meat.

   The men moved towards it and smelt the meat.

   'This must surely be Death,' they said

   And let the canoe pass by and vanish.

   Time passed.

   Until one day the second canoe appeared.

   In it a young man.

   Strange and alien, but who waved and greeted them like a
    brother.

   They waded out and drew the boat in to the river bank.

   Embraced the stranger, asked him who he was.

He was Death.
When the creator arrived in the third canoe
He saw there was nothing he could do for the men.
The trees had waited for him
They will never die.
The stones had waited for him
They will live for ever.
The snakes had waited for him
And when they grew old they shed their skin and were
    young again.
But the men had welcomed Death like a long-lost brother.
And he, smiling, took them one by one into his arms.
(WEST *exits*.)
(*The* INDIANS *pass the gourd around and drink, laughing and
excited, as the* WOMEN *prepare the food*.)

Thirteen

The guerrilla hideout. WEST, *handcuffed, alone, reading a Portuguese
edition of* The Godfather. CARLOS *enters, beaming, carrying two
bowls of soup and some bread.*

CARLOS: Good evening.

WEST: Hello. You're looking very cheerful.

CARLOS: Yes, I've had a good day, very successful operation.

WEST: Really?

CARLOS: Yes, I rang the police this morning and told them the
American Embassy was being attacked by a gang of thugs
disguised as an army unit and then I rang army head-
quarters and told them the American Embassy was being
attacked by a gang of thugs in police uniform. Then I went
and watched from a safe distance. Most satisfactory.

WEST: You mean it worked?

CARLOS: Three dead, a dozen or so wounded and a certain
amount of damage to property.

    (*Silence*.)

WEST: Well, how nice for you.

CARLOS: Yes, it was.

WEST: Why do you people always blame the Americans for everything?

CARLOS: You know as well as I do the Americans were behind the coup in 1964, and they were behind it because their profits were being threatened, and now they bribe the ruling classes to make sure their profits aren't threatened again. The American public knows their government gives aid to underdeveloped countries, unless they're communist of course, in which case they prefer to ship over a few tons of napalm, but what they don't know is that nearly all the aid has strings attached, and what they also don't know is that twice as much money comes out in profit as goes in in aid. Why do you think the corporations make two, three, sometimes ten times as much profit in Latin America as they do in their home markets? You may think all's fair in love and commerce, but some of us take it personally when our children starve to death so that somebody in Detroit or Pittsburgh can buy themselves a third car.

WEST: That's a ludicrously oversimplified way of putting it.

CARLOS: Well, as it so happens, it's a ludicrously oversimplified process, starving. You don't get enough food to eat and, by an absurdly oversimplified foible of nature, it makes you die. And it can be very aggravating when you think to yourself that the excess profits which ought to have been ploughed back into your country so you might have stood a chance of getting a bite to eat have gone towards installing a telex in the interests of business efficiency. It can be a terrible setback to your notions of international brotherhood.

WEST: Well, these things develop slowly . . .

CARLOS: We haven't got time for slowly. We need fast.

WEST: But a lot of these things just can't be done fast.

CARLOS: They can't be done at all, as long as the Americans have their teeth in our neck. Don't think I'm so stupid as to be against them just because they're Americans. If it wasn't them, it'd be someone else. It's just that they're the most powerful at the moment. Before them it was you.

64

WEST: Me?

CARLOS: You. England. You bled us empty all through the seventeenth and eighteenth centuries. Or rather Portugal bled us and you bled Portugal.

WEST: I thought Portugal was supposed to be our oldest ally.

CARLOS: Of course. If I had you round the throat squeezing you dry for hundreds of years, you'd be my oldest ally.

WEST: Well, it's hardly my fault.

CARLOS: That's it. Nothing's ever anyone's fault. Millions of dollars flow out of the country, quite spontaneously, to the amazement of all. By some freak statistical whim, 3 per cent of the population of an underdeveloped country find themselves controlling most of the wealth and look on bewildered as it slips from their nerveless fingers and fortuitously lands in a numbered Swiss bank account. How can it be anyone's fault?

WEST: None of it ever lands in my numbered Swiss bank account.

CARLOS: Think what you're missing, you silly man. My father has three.

WEST: That's very interesting.

CARLOS: For you, maybe. Not for me. I don't get on very cordially with my father, he being well to the right of Caligula. Apart from counting his money, he has only two enthusiasms: Vasco da Gama football club and the Death Squad.

WEST: What does he think about you?

CARLOS: He thinks I see everything exactly the way he does. (*Silence.*)

WEST: Somebody I know was killed by the Death Squad not so long ago.

CARLOS: Well well.

WEST: So the story goes, anyway. He wasn't anyone we knew very well, a friend of a friend in England, we met him two or three times. He was a homosexual, so of course when the bank posted him to Rio, he thought it was his birthday. They just broke in one night, took him to some obscure favela and shot him. Because he was homosexual, we were told.

CARLOS: Oh, yes, the Death Squad disapproves of immorality.

E   65

WEST: Well, in my opinion, their puritan zeal was rather undermined by the fact that they sexually assaulted him before they killed him.

CARLOS: It's a very tragic tale.

WEST: Yes, I think it is quite.

CARLOS: Well, after all the things that have been done to friends of mine in the last year or two, you must forgive me if I'm not moved to tears by some garbled story about some foreign faggot.

WEST: Oh.

CARLOS: Listen, I won't go into details about it . . . yes, I will, I will go into details about it, I will, I'll tell you what happened to a friend of mine, a girl of seventeen called Maria, a philosophy student, who had only the very remotest connection with us. She was a very quiet, thoughtful girl and she lived with her grandmother in Urca. Last September, they arrived in the middle of the night, and since it was a political offence she was suspected of, they naturally started off by raping her, right there in front of the old woman. Then they hauled her off for a few days on the Ilha das Flores and gave her all the usual treatment, more rape, electric shock, hanging her upside-down on the parrot perch and beating her, all that. She hasn't recovered from it and I don't think she ever will. She's still under treatment. She sent a message to us saying she never wanted to see any of us ever again. Mind you, it wouldn't do us much good if we did go to see her, because they gave her another piece of standard treatment, humorously referred to as the telephone, which consists of punching the ears of the victims as they hang upside-down. They broke her eardrums. She's completely deaf.

WEST: Horrible.

CARLOS: You see, countries like ours operate their own version of the Welfare State. Instead of wasting a lot of money trying to reform and rehabilitate psychopaths, sex maniacs, thugs and sadists, we give them a uniform and a good salary and a title like the Death Squad, or the C.C.C., or the Metros, or the C.R.S. and let them use their skills for society's

benefit. (*He sees* WEST'*s dubious expression.*) Don't think there
aren't hundreds of people in every country who'd jump at
the chance to belong to that kind of organisation, who'd
love to spend an evening throwing beggars in the river or
ramming a broken-off bottleneck up any pretty middle-class
girl with a few vague ideals about improving the lot of the
workers. And don't think there aren't thousands of people
in every country who'd sleep more comfortably in their
beds if they knew that kind of thing was going on. And the
unity those people have, the unity of hatred, the wonderfully
simple level of their ideas! Whereas we, my God, we poor
old nit-picking intellectuals, I sometimes think we spend all
our strengths and all our energy bickering over points of
doctrine like a gaggle of old nuns discussing the Immaculate
Conception in a brothel.

WEST: I don't see how you can hope to achieve anything.

CARLOS: We will, in the end.

WEST: You'd need a miracle.

CARLOS: Anything can happen. Suppose there was nuclear war
between America and Russia. I don't expect you know this,
but by some quirk of the trade winds or whatever, Brazil
would suffer less fall-out than any other country in the
world. Then we might be able to make some progress, like
we did in the First World War when the Imperialists got off
our backs, we might even turn into that superpower the
generals keep prattling about. You see, we always look on
the bright side. We're not like Lady Britannia, sinking
sedately beneath the waves and stolidly replacing one
reactionary government with another even more reactionary
government; our country is so vast that the most terrible
things can happen without anyone even noticing—but it's
also young enough to change in the most radical and
unexpected ways.

(*Silence.*)

WEST: I remember being in a little town on the Araguaia, sitting
by the river, waiting for a boat which was needless to say
several hours late. I was watching the children, who were
going up and down the river-bank in groups of two or three,

67

very active. I couldn't see what they were up to at first, but after a time I realised they were hunting out anything that was alive down by the river, small animals, reptiles, insects, anything they could find, and torturing it to death. Naturally I, sitting there like an idiot in my tropical ducks, was something of a centre of attraction for them, and they kept bringing me little offerings, like a worm sliced into six wriggling pieces or quite a large lizard with all its legs pulled off. They went on for hours, dozens of them, that's all they were doing.

(*He breaks off, reflecting. Brief silence.*)

CARLOS: Well, what else is there for them to do, comrade?

BLACKOUT

Fourteen

Ground plan as Scene Seven.

INVESTIGATOR: And you attacked did you
           When you reached the village?

PEREIRA: No.
        Not right off.
        We stayed where we were until nightfall.
        Then during the night
        We crawled to the edge of the village
        And waited for the dawn.
        Being the best shot
        My job was to start the attack off
        By killing the chief.
        Well in the morning
        They all got on with what they were doing
        Which was building some hut
        And more or less straight away
        I picked out the chief
        A tall man
        Who was leaning against a rock doing nothing.

I got him first go.
Then Chico gave them a burst of his sub-machine gun
And we all charged.
It was over in five minutes.
All that time struggling through the jungle
And in five minutes
It was all over.

INVESTIGATOR: All over?

PEREIRA: Well not quite.
Not quite.

INVESTIGATOR: What do you mean?

PEREIRA: Well now we get to the cruel part
Nothing to do with me
I tried to stop it happening.

INVESTIGATOR: What?
What did you try to stop?

PEREIRA: There was a girl.
A young girl.
We thought we'd got everyone you see
Then we heard this screaming and yelling
And we found a child of about five
With this young girl who was trying to hush it up.
Chico was very pleased.
He led them out into the centre of the village.
Here we go he said.
I said we should take them back with us.
He shook his head.
No he said we're supposed to kill them all
All these animals.
Then he grabbed the little boy threw him on the ground
And shot him in the head.
She just stood there
Not making a sound
Stark naked
Pretty little thing.
All right he said he said Pedro
Give me your machete.
Listen I said don't kill her

I mean here's all of us
Not seen a woman for six weeks.
Find your own women he said.
He looked funny.
He led her over to a tree
And got Pedro to help him hang her upside-down
Legs apart.
Then he chopped her in half.
Afterwards he said you can have her now if you like
She's all yours.

(*Silence.*)

INVESTIGATOR: Then you left did you?

PEREIRA: You bet.
We threw all the bodies in the river
And got the hell out as fast as we could.

INVESTIGATOR: And you got back all right?

PEREIRA: Yes sure
But that's when all the trouble started
I was telling you about.

INVESTIGATOR: Tell me about it again.

PEREIRA: Well when we got back
They were furious with us for having taken so long
And they refused to pay us.
They said they weren't going to waste their time with us
any more.
They were going back to the old more efficient methods
Such as poisoned candy
And sending them infected blankets.
I said it was a scandal
But he said that was the Company's final decision
And it wasn't for him to query it.
Now I ask you be fair
It's not right is it?
All that sweat and slog and hard work
For nothing.
I'd have thought they might have given us a bonus
But no
The Company won't even pay me what it promised.

70

INVESTIGATOR: How much was that?
PEREIRA: Fifteen dollars.

BLACKOUT

Fifteen

The CHIEF *sits, alone, on a stool, in front of the central post, his bow across his knees.*

WEST *appears.*

WEST: The life after death.

Long ago there was a boy who fell in love with a star.
He called to her every night and told her of his love
Until one night she answered him inviting him to join her
By climbing a certain palm tree.

The boy climbed the tree and reached the desolate fields
  of heaven
And for many weeks he was entirely happy
But sometimes as he lay with his love he was disturbed
  by strange sounds
The murmur of distant celebration.

The star begged him to take no notice of this distraction
But soon his curiosity overcame his love
And he set off alone across the fields
Towards the sound of the flutes.

What he had heard was the endless dance of the dead.
What he saw was the numberless tribe of the dead
Fresh corpses rotting bodies skeletons
Dancing to the cruel music of death.

The boy ran from the field of the dead in horror
Fled from the eye of the great hawk
Who sat in the dead bones of a dead tree guarding his
  prisoners

Eating their putrid flesh.

The boy ran to the palm tree and began to climb down
    towards the earth
But the star saw him and called after him: 'You cannot
    escape. You will soon return.'
And a few days later the boy had wasted away
And his body returned to the dance.

Before he died he told the people what he had seen
And now it is known
That although the stars smile down and speak of the
    beauty of heaven
There is no rest and no joy in the field of the dead.
(WEST *exits*.)

(*Music. The* INDIANS *appear and dispose themselves on either
side of the stage, facing the centre. Then an* INDIAN *carrying a
bow enters, leading a* GIRL, *who walks with her right hand on
his shoulder. The* GIRL, *who has just been brought out of
seclusion, wears feathers in her hair, beads and cloth binding
round the upper part of her calves. Her hair grows down
covering her face. In her left hand, she carries a gourd full of
pequi nuts. The* INDIAN *leading her stops when she is directly
in front of the* CHIEF, *and without taking her hand off his
shoulder, she leans back as far as possible in a graceful
movement and empties the nuts on the ground in front of the
CHIEF. They move forward a couple of paces and stop again.
A young* INDIAN *approaches and takes the feathers from her
hair, her beads and the binding from her legs. The other
INDIANS close in around the CHIEF and begin helping themselves
to the pequi nuts as the* LIGHTS DIM.)

Sixteen

The guerrilla hideout. WEST, *handcuffed, kneels with his back towards the audience as* CARLOS *finishes off cutting his hair with a pair of nail-scissors.*

CARLOS: There we are. Very nice. I'm afraid we don't have any double mirrors so you'll just have to take my word for it. (WEST *turns round carefully, sits on the bed facing* CARLOS. *He pats at his hair.*)

WEST: Thanks.

CARLOS: Well, we can't let you out looking like a tramp, can we? The bourgeois press would be saying we didn't know how to conduct ourselves like gentlemen.

WEST: Now all I need is a bath.

CARLOS: More difficult to arrange, I'm afraid. (*He sniffs delicately.*) I think you'll be all right without. I'll give you a slosh of my capitalist after-shave.

WEST: Well, thank you.

(CARLOS *brushes a knot of hair off* WEST's *shoulder.*)

CARLOS: I must say I'm very pleased with that. Who says intellectuals can't work with their hands?

WEST: Yes, if you fall on hard times in Cuba, you can always apply for a job trimming Fidel's beard.

(CARLOS *frowns.*)

Sorry.

(CARLOS *shrugs. Pause.*)

Are you looking forward to going to Cuba?

CARLOS (*sharply*): Yes, of course I am. (*Pause.*) It's very serious to leave your country and not know if you will ever be able to come back. But it will be very good to wake up in the morning and not have to worry about whether you're going to get through the day without being arrested, tortured or killed.

WEST: Why are you going exactly? If it's not a . . .

CARLOS: I don't think I can talk to you about that.

WEST: All right.

CARLOS: I . . . The truth is, I'm not a very valuable guerrilla. First thing, I'm a terrible shot. We go and practise, you know, on those machines in amusement arcades, but it's hopeless, I'm no good, they all say I couldn't hit an elephant if it was sitting on my knee. And we have

73

differences, sometimes, you know, about matters of principle. Certain disagreements.

WEST: What about?

CARLOS: Matters of principle. Tactics. (*Longish pause.*) Some of us, some of us believe that excessive terrorist violence is counterproductive. For instance, you remember when McNamara visited, we set off a bomb outside Sears Roebuck in São Paolo. That did no good. I mean, who knows except for us that McNamara owns shares in Sears Roebuck? All people knew was that their nearest cheap store was closed for two weeks and they were very angry about it. I think we have to be very careful not to use the methods of the enemy to defeat the enemy. It's essential for us to use violence, of course, but we must be very sure that every act of violence we commit is clear and . . . progressive.

WEST: I take it you aren't opposed to kidnapping.

CARLOS: No. Certainly, it's regrettable, but how else are we going to get our comrades out of the torture-chambers?

WEST: Yes, I can see how trying it must be for you.

CARLOS: There's no point in our talking about this. You're an intelligent man, I know you understand.
(*Silence.*)

WEST: So they're sending you off to have another think.

CARLOS: Well, we had a lot of arguments, discussions that is, and in the end they said, Carlos, you're a man who can't hit a brick wall at three paces, why don't you go and set your thoughts down in a book for us? (*Pause. Then, almost convincingly.*) We decided it would be more useful.
(*Silence.*)

WEST: Tomorrow, then?

CARLOS: Yes, all being well.

WEST: Amazing.
(*Silence.*)

CARLOS: I think I should tell you something, I was told not to mention it but I don't see what difference it can make. Your wife has gone back to England.

WEST: Oh. Oh, well.

CARLOS: So you won't see her tomorrow. In a few days.

WEST: I see.
(*Silence.*)
CARLOS: Are you, erm, happily married, are you?
WEST: Very. (*Pause.*) Not very. So-so. All right, you know.
We're used to each other.
CARLOS: Children?
WEST: No. (*Pause.*) What about you, are you married?
CARLOS (*laughing*): No. Not for me. I'm much too fond of women
to get married. That's another thing that's caused some . . .
disputes in the past. Some people think my private life is
self-indulgent and dangerous. Too many books about Mata
Hari, you see, they all think I'm liable to become besotted
with some sinister foreign whore who'll make me pour out
all my secrets. I explained to them that on the contrary
comrades who weren't at all successful with women would
be far more susceptible to that kind of thing, but many of
them didn't seem to find that a sympathetic point of view.
(*Pause.*) Of course, what they disapprove of most is that I
have a terrible weakness for American girls.
WEST: Well, that is rather heretical, isn't it?
CARLOS: Not at all. Infiltrating the enemy, I call it. No, the thing
is, I just love American girls of about twenty. They're
always so enthusiastic and fresh and responsive and eager,
beautiful skin, wide eyes, wonderful mixture of alertness
and ignorance. Always so healthy. Question is, what
happens to them?
WEST: I'm afraid I don't know anything about it.
CARLOS: If I had to give a definition of capitalism I would say:
the process whereby American girls turn into American
women.
WEST (*laughs*): Capitalism, there's a quaint old word. Don't hear
it nearly so often nowadays. I remember when I was much
younger, I was posted in Venice, at the Palazzo Dario. Used
to hear a lot about capitalism in those days, and I used to
think this is where it started and this is what it is: a lot of
sinking palaces.
CARLOS: Well, that's very good. But it gives you away, you see,
far too romantic. If you want a city that really tells you

75

what capitalism is all about, look at Brasilia. Designed by a Marxist architect as a city for the people and a city without slums. Then the property speculators get going, and before you know where you are the workers can't afford to live in the apartment blocks they're building. Well, they don't want to dirty up that sparkling white city, so the answer is, build slums in a big circle twenty miles outside the city and bus the workers in every day and watch a city for the people turn into a city where the workers have to construct the class barriers with their own hands.

WEST: I know you see the problems. The thing is, I just don't believe you have the solutions.

CARLO (*amiably*): You people believe in what you have. The rich believe in money, the intelligent believe in intelligence, the powerful believe in power, the Army believes in strength, the Church believes in morality. But you really mustn't expect that to apply to everyone. You really shouldn't expect the oppressed to believe in misery and the starving to believe in hunger.

WEST: It's been a very long time since I expected anything.

BLACKOUT

Seventeen

A bar, though what we see can hardly be dignified with that title. The customers are all Indians, 'integrados', drinking from bottles, dressed in shabby cast-offs. Some are lying senseless in the familiar attitudes of Skid Row. Others have that lost, remote, melancholy expression of the Indian for whom nothing has replaced the tribal organisation from which he has been divorced. They swig morosely at their bottles.

AMERICAN VOICE: Take a gamble in the Mato Grosso!

For as little as twelve dollars an acre, you can join Prince Rainier of Monaco, several famous Hollywood stars and a host of international celebrities as the owner of a fabulous Amazon Adventure Estate in Brazil's most mysterious and exotic region.

You may find yourself the possessor of one of Brazil's
fabled diamond mines, an oil baron or a manganese king
—anything may happen as you stake yourself out a share
in the inexhaustible resources of this hitherto virtually
unexplored nation within a nation.
Brazil's new progressive government, friendly to the U.S.,
has accorded top priority to the development of these vast
jungle territories—and its new roadbuilding program
will open up the area as never before.
In the next few years the development of Brazil's interior
is going to be very big business indeed—and we want you
to have a piece of the action.
Don't forget, too, that labor is plentiful and can cost as
little as seven U.S. cents per unit per hour.
We all of us have just a little bit of the Frontier Spirit in
our bones, don't we?
Yours should be telling you now to invest in the land of the
future and find your own personal El Dorado.
Huge profits are to be made!

Eighteen

Ground plan as Scene Five.
WEST: So you really don't think things are improving at all?
CRAWSHAW: Well, they may be. I can only go by what I've seen
myself. I mean, I was in the Xingu only a couple of months
ago, 25th May 1970, I remember the date because it was
the day before my birthday, and they flew in the remnants
of the Beiços-de-Pau tribe. They're called that because they
wear those, you know, lip-discs. They lived up by the river
Arinos, and as far as we know, that's to say at the beginning
of the year, there were about 400 of them left. There had,
of course, been far more than that, but a few years ago, an
expedition came up the river and left them a few sacks of
food mixed with arsenic. Anyhow, after a great deal of red

77

tape and nonsense it was decided to fly them into the Xingu, as it was obvious they didn't stand a chance of surviving where they were. So then it began. The rescue operation. Phase one was the measles epidemic, because as chance would have it, one of the rescue party was carrying measles. Only 109 of them survived it, but there we are. Phase two was the publicity stunt, in which four of the Indians were flown to Rio to meet the press. Unfortunately that didn't work out too well either, because three of them died in Rio. Phase three was transferring them to the transit camp. Now that hadn't been thought out too thoroughly, because what they did was drive them down overnight in open trucks, not altogether taking into account the fact that the Indians were naked and it was the middle of the winter. As a result of which another 65 of them died. This made the logistics of phase four, which was actually flying them into the Xingu, a good deal easier, but even so they weren't as careful as they might have been, and the 41 survivors were bundled into an unpressurised cargo 'plane and set off on the last stage of their great adventure. I was there when the plane landed at dawn at Posto Leonardo. We lifted them all out and laid them on the ground, the corpses to one side and the living to another, although it was by no means easy to distinguish. In the end we found that 24 of them were what you might technically call alive. It was quite cold. They lay on the ground without moving, they didn't move at all even when the ants began crawling up their nostrils and into their eyes. I tried passing my hand in front of their eyes, but they didn't blink, and the eyes didn't move at all, they gave no indication of seeing. They were lost. They were all lost. (*Long pause.*) It just so happens I witnessed that, but I could have told you about any one of a dozen tribes, same story, different details. It's strange, when I was in England, I didn't seem to be able to turn on the television without seeing some impassioned programme about some threatened animal species. I mean, I've got nothing against that, it's just that everyone knows the blue whale and the white rhino are in trouble. But who's ever heard of the Beiços-de-Pau or

78

the Pacaas Novas or the Trumai?

WEST: People are sentimental about animals.

CRAWSHAW: Well, God knows, people are sentimental about
Indians as well, and that's no help either, all those Noble
Savage boys. I mean, I'd be the first to admit they show as
much aggression, greed, superstition and cowardice as the
next man. It's just that in their own terms they've provided
themselves with solutions to all their immediate problems,
and that makes them very well balanced, very relaxed and
very happy.

WEST: And very innocent.

CRAWSHAW: Not if you mean unsophisticated, no. Only if you
mean free of guilt. (*Pause.*) I think it's partly the way the
children are brought up. The tribe I was with must have
used some method of contraception, possibly an abortifacient,
although I never managed to find out how they worked it.
Anyway, the women had children more or less once every
four years and for the first four years of the child's life its
mother was never out of its sight. I used to watch the
women grinding manioc with their children slung on their
shoulders, and the children would urinate or defecate right
there, all down their mother's side, and the mother wouldn't
react at all, she'd just smile sometimes or not smile and
carry on working.

WEST: Extraordinary.

(*Silence. Then* MRS. WEST *rises.*)

MRS. WEST: Well, Miles, I'm sure you two will excuse me if I
take myself off to bed now.

(CRAWSHAW *and* WEST *both rise.*)

CRAWSHAW: I'm sorry, I've probably stayed too long and talked
too much.

MRS. WEST: Not at all. Please don't go on my account.

WEST: No, have another brandy.

CRAWSHAW: Erm . . .

(*He is about to refuse, but* MRS. WEST *advances on him, hand
outstretched, as* WEST *splashes more brandy into his glass.*)

MRS. WEST (*shaking* CRAWSHAW's *hand*): It was very nice to see
you this evening, Miles.

79

CRAWSHAW: Yes. Thank you very much for dinner.

MRS. WEST: I'm afraid the rice pudding was absolutely disgusting.

CRAWSHAW: No, it was very nice.

MRS. WEST: I expect we'll see you again soon.

CRAWSHAW: Hope so.

MRS. WEST: Good night then.

CRAWSHAW: Good night.

WEST: See you later, dear.

> (MRS. WEST *exits.* CRAWSHAW *and* WEST *sit down, and* CRAWSHAW *sips nervously at his brandy.*)

CRAWSHAW: I must be on my way in a minute.

WEST: No, don't go. There's no need to go. I'm very interested.

CRAWSHAW: The thing is . . . (*He breaks off.*)

WEST: Go on. Go on talking.

CRAWSHAW: The thing is they know it, they know what they've got and you haven't. (*Pause.*) A year or so ago, I spent some time, a couple of months, with one of the nomadic tribes. And they had, I mean they owned nothing at all. They kept moving, they fed themselves on what they could catch, lizards, snakes, rats, whatever. They cooked what they had in the evening, then they put out the fire and slept in the ashes, all huddled together in each other's arms to keep warm. They had no home, no clothes and no possessions. Eventually the time came for me to leave them, and I explained it to them; it was a very emotional moment, we were all very upset about it. I used to sleep, rather prudishly, in a sleeping-bag, a little way off from them and that night, half-an-hour or so after we'd all settled down, I heard them weeping. After a bit, I got up and went over and sat near them. I said: you mustn't cry because I'm leaving, I shall come back some time. Then one of them said: we are not sad for ourselves, that we shall be without you; we are sad for you, that you can bear to leave us. You see they look into your eyes and they know it all.

BLACKOUT

Nineteen

The guerrilla hideout. WEST, *handcuffed, looks furious.* CARLOS *paces uneasily up and down.*

CARLOS: Well, look, I'm very sorry, that's all I can say.

WEST: It's not enough, I want to know why.

CARLOS: I told you, there's been a hitch. A minor hitch, which means we have to delay everything for twenty-four hours.

WEST: Listen, I've been very patient cooped up here all these weeks listening to your dreary propaganda, but there's just so much I can take.

CARLOS: I'm very sorry, it was my fault, I should never have said anything to you about it yesterday. I thought you'd be pleased to know.

WEST: I was, of course I was, I thought it was true.

CARLOS: It's only another twenty-four hours. I promise you you'll be out tomorrow.

WEST: You'd better give me that in writing.

CARLOS: We all have to suffer for the cause, comrade.

WEST: I don't see why I should suffer for your wretched cause.

CARLOS: Because it's essential.

WEST: That's a matter of opinion.

CARLOS: It's a matter of fact.

WEST: Look, as far as I'm concerned, there are causes in Brazil which are far more essential. Like, for instance the extermination of the people who used to own this country. That seems to me far more important than replacing one authoritarian government with another.

CARLOS: Is that what you think we're trying to do?

WEST: Well, I hardly imagined you had parliamentary democracy in mind.

CARLOS: Whatever makes you think democracy would be any use to us? Mm? Democracy is a luxury for countries rich enough so it doesn't matter who they elect. You don't think we're risking our lives so we can put in some bumbling idiot who'll waste all his energy trying not to upset anyone? We're fighting this war on behalf of the people. What could be more democratic than that?

WEST: Letting the people choose.

CARLOS: Don't be absurd. How do you expect people to choose when all they're worried about is where the next crust of bread is coming from? There are children of eight on the streets of Rio offering themselves to anyone in a suit, you think they're going to turn into good Democrats? You make me laugh. All this crap about the Indians, it's just romantic bourgeois sentimentality. Listen, there are ninety million people in this country, and there aren't enough Indians left to fill up Maracana football stadium. So you say, look after the Indians, after all, poor things, it used to be their country, didn't it, and they'll never cause much trouble, because there are hardly any of them left, and they're not interested anyway. Look after the Indians, you say, but for Christ's sake don't look after the ninety million, or you never know what they might start wanting. All your liberal hearts bleed at the thought of those poor naked savages fading away, but it never begins to dribble across your apology for a mind that half a million children under five starved to death in Brazil last year.

WEST: That is a complete perversion of my point of view.

(CARLOS *responds with sounds mimicking West's pomposity.*)

(*Indignant.*) You people are all the same.

CARLOS (*enraged*): So are you people.

(*He storms out.* WEST *sits, frowning, staring blankly into space. A moment later,* CARLOS *returns with the chess board.*)

Better we don't have any more discussions, don't you think? Better we just play chess. (*Pause. He begins setting up the board.*) You might even win this time.

WEST: I don't really feel like it just now.

(CARLOS *goes on calmly distributing the pieces.*)

CARLOS: I don't have anything particular against you. It's just I can't help trying.

WEST: What do you mean?

82

CARLOS: Che said, if a man is honest, you can make a
revolutionary out of him. You seem honest enough.
(*He selects two pawns and holds his closed fists out towards*
WEST. *Long pause. Finally* WEST *indicates one, and* CARLOS
opens his fist to show the white pawn. WEST *takes it from him.*)
Off you go.
(WEST *makes an opening move.*)
WEST: I've a feeling I am going to win.

BLACKOUT

Twenty

The CHIEF *and his* WIFE *sit, waiting.* WEST *appears.*
WEST: Origin of the masks.
In the middle of the night
After a bad day's hunting and hungry to bed
A man heard something moving around near his hut
And running out found a giant paca which he killed.

There was enough meat for everyone in the village
But two did not join in the feast
A woman who that night was giving birth
And her husband.

The next day when the men had set off hunting
A devil wearing a bark mask appeared in the woman's hut
He told her that the villagers had killed and eaten his son
And that he must be revenged.

She and her husband and child he said would be spared
And told her to gather the bark from a certain tree
That night the devils came and killed every villager
But the three who hid their faces behind the bark.

83

Now it is known that the wearing of the bark masks
Is certain protection against the devils.
For who seeing his own image his own skin
Could destroy his own kind?

(WEST *exits.*)

(*Music. Two* INDIANS *appear, playing ten-foot flutes and
dancing. Behind them, with their right hands on the* MEN's
shoulders, two GIRLS *dance in time. They circle and weave
around the posts and across the stage. The* CHIEF *rises and
moves behind the posts. As he does so, the other* INDIANS *rise
and join the dance. The* CHIEF *emerges from behind the posts
wearing a mask, dancing his own dance. The ceremony is
reaching a climax of excitement and exhilaration.*)

(*Cutting through this the sound of a light aircraft. The*
INDIANS *falter, continue, falter again, and, as the sound of the
aeroplane increases in intensity, gradually stop. The
'plane is now overhead.*)

(*It drops bombs.*)

(*Explosions, panic, chaos. The sound of the 'plane
diminishes, then increases again as it turns and flies back over
the village even lower.*)

(*More bombs.*)

(*Screams of pain and fear.*)

BLACKOUT

Twenty One

The guerrilla hideout. WEST, *handcuffed, contemplating the chess-
board.* CARLOS *watching him. A knock at the door.* CARLOS *gets up and
leaves the room. Long pause, during which* WEST *gives out a little
grunt of pleasure and makes a move. Then the door bursts open and*
CARLOS *re-enters, white and tense. In his hand, though at first con-
cealed from* WEST, *the pistol with silencer.* WEST *looks up, triumphant,
indicates the chess-board.*

WEST: Pick the bones out of that.

CARLOS: I . . .

WEST: I think I've . . . (*He sees the gun and breaks off suddenly.*) What's erm . . . ?

CARLOS: I . . . (*He levels the pistol at* WEST.)

WEST (*feebly*): Don't.

CARLOS: Sorry.

> (*He shoots* WEST *three times.* WEST *slumps grotesquely to the floor, still dangling from his handcuff.* CARLOS *looks at him for a second, desolate. Then, from outside, the wail of a police siren.* CARLOS *starts, then rushes out. A hail of machine-gun fire in the* BLACKOUT.)
>
> (*Fanfares, reminiscent of the opening of a TV news bulletin. A white frontcloth drops in. On it are projected, one by one, overlapping, innumerable photographs of* WEST, *black and white, colour, family snaps, headlines in several languages, until the whole cloth is covered with images of* WEST.)

Twenty Two

The frontcloth rises to reveal a bloody heap of Indian bodies. Silence. Then a groan of pain.

TWO MEN *enter with sub-machine-guns, one, as is clear from his goggles and flying-jacket, the pilot of the 'plane, the other his co-pilot.*

One of the Indians in the pile of bodies onstage groans, and begins painfully to rise to his feet. It is the CHIEF, *still wearing his mask.*

One of the men shoots down the CHIEF *and fires a burst into the heap of bodies, then they pass across the stage and off. A cry followed by another burst of machine-gun fire offstage. Silence.*

The MEN *return, looking well pleased. The* PILOT *pauses, tucks the gun under his arm, produces a packet of cigarettes, offers one to his companion, takes one himself and lights them. Pause. Then he throws the box of matches to his companion who nods and leaves the stage. A moment later, he returns without his gun, but with two torches headed* with rags soaked in kerosene. *He lights one and hands it to the* PILOT, *then lights the other. They leave the stage in the direction of the village.*

Silence. An animal cry, another soft groan, the light drone of flies. The crackle of flames.

Effect of flames as the LIGHTS DIM *to* BLACKOUT.